SILVER BURDETT PROFESSIONAL PUBLICATIONS

Mathematics Instruction in Early Childhood

Mathematics Instruction in the Elementary Grades

Building Foundations in Elementary Mathematics

Changing Behavior Patterns—How and Why

Classroom Teacher Series

Improving Behavior:
100 Applications for the Elementary Classroom

Ideas for Teaching Social Studies

Hints for the Classroom Teacher

Mathematics Games for Classroom Use

100 Applications for the Elementary Classroom

SILVER BURDETT PROFESSIONAL PUBLICATIONS

IMPROVING BEHAVIOR

Nick Kostiuk, Ed. D.

Eli Barkan, Ed. M.

John Rocco, Ed. D.

SILVER BURDETT COMPANY
Morristown, New Jersey
Glenview, Illinois • Palo Alto • Dallas • Atlanta

ACKNOWLEDGEMENTS

Grateful acknowledgements are extended to David Reckless, William Stevens, and Selma Tolins for editorial assistance and to Patricia Rampulla and Charles J. Ross for assistance with the artwork.

Illustrations by Richard Stalzer

Cover design by Tonna Associates, Inc.

© 1979 SILVER BURDETT COMPANY.

All rights reserved.

Printed in the United States of America.

This publication, or parts thereof, may not be reproduced in any form by photographic, electrostatic, mechanical or any other method, for any use, including information storage and retrieval, without written permission from the publisher.

ISBN 0-382-02609-8

Library of Congress Card Number: 78-56760

A Word from the Authors

If you are an elementary school teacher who has a Michael, Richard, or Stephen in your classroom who is "turned off" from learning and whose disruptive behavior keeps others from learning, this book is for you.

If you are the teacher who has hyperactive children, withdrawn children, slow learners, aggressive children, or children with learning disabilities, this book is for you.

If you are the highly creative teacher who is looking for additional ways of perking-up or motivating youngsters and preventing crises from arising in your classroom, this book is for you.

Improving Behavior: 100 Applications for the Elementary Classroom is written for the busy teacher who wants practical ideas and suggestions quickly without having to read a considerable amount of technical terminology. As the title suggests, the book contains one hundred practical applications in behavior modification. These practical suggestions have come from elementary school teachers who have used the techniques successfully with children of varying ages, temperaments, and problems in kindergarten through grade six. A Bonus section provides five additional Applications.

For easy use, the book has been organized like a cookbook. Each application is a self contained unit, and is like a recipe for the improvement of behavior and learning in a classroom. Each application has a title. The titles are arranged in alphabetical order for quick reference. A Classified Index on pages xiv to xvi lists the applications according to the behavior pattern to be modified. A Grade Level Index is given on pages xvii to xx.

Each of the one hundred five practical applications is divided into three parts:

Situation,
describing a typical classroom problem that a teacher might face.

Strategy,
a step-by-step, easily followed procedure for coping effectively with the situation or preventing future ones from arising.

Rationale,
the reasons for using a particular strategy. The strategies involve processes that are practical, positive in scope, educationally sound, and fun for children, yet do not require the expenditure of vast sums of money. They are equally applicable to urban, suburban, and rural areas. In addition, the strategies have multiple uses. They are not restricted to the particular situations mentioned. They can be expanded to other situations and used with children of differing personalities, ages, and grade levels, as well as in the teaching of different subjects or disciplines. For example, although a strategy is suggested for an aggressive child, it might also have practical applications for a withdrawn child, or one with a learning disability. Creative teachers will be able to take the one hundred practical applications and use them in many hundreds of other situations. They should also be able to develop many of their own behavioral strategies, similar to those in the book, thereby giving children even greater opportunities for success.

Although *Improving Behavior* has been written for elementary school classroom teachers, it has many practical applications which can be of infinite value to principals, parents, counselors, psychologists, social workers, nurses, special education personnel, and other individuals who are in daily contact with children.

The Authors

Dr. Nick Kostiuk has been an elementary school teacher, an elementary school principal, and a college professor. His public school experiences have included working with innovative programs for children in nursery school through grade eight in both urban and suburban school systems. On the college level he has worked with both graduate and undergraduate students at Indiana University of Pennsylvania and at Pennsylvania State University. He is presently principal of the Cold Spring School in Willow Grove, Pennsylvania.

Mr. Eli Barkan has been an elementary school teacher, an elementary school guidance counselor, a school psychologist, a coordinator of a reading improvement program for migrant children in Florida, and a coordinator of a special education center in Willow Grove, Pennsylvania. Mr. Barkan was the founding director of the first clinic for children with learning disabilities in Winnepeg, Canada. He is currently in private practice in Hatboro, Pennsylvania.

Dr. John Rocco has been an elementary school teacher, an elementary school principal, and a director of continuing education at a community college. He currently serves as a professor at Rider College, an adjunct professor at Rutgers University, and is a former mayor of the community of Cherry Hill in New Jersey.

Dr. Kostiuk and Mr. Barkan currently serve as behavior modification consultants for various school districts and universities. Dr. Rocco is a consultant and lecturer in humanistic education. The experiences of the three authors have been combined in this book to provide teachers with a practical resource that will enable them to deal more effectively with a variety of classroom situations.

Contents

A WORD FROM THE AUTHORS		v
ABOUT THE AUTHORS		vii
CLASSIFIED INDEX		xiv
GRADE LEVEL INDEX		xvii
INTRODUCTION		xxi

ONE HUNDRED PRACTICAL APPLICATIONS

Title	Grade Level	Page
After School Helper	5–6	2
The Anecdote	4–6	3
Aquarium	1–3	4
Beat Your Own Score	3–6	5
Befriending A Classmate	5–6	7
The Big Clap	2–5	8
The Bookshelf	3–6	9
Breakfast In School	2–6	10
The Buddies	3–6	11
Bulletin Board Committee Row Game	4–6	12
Carbon Paper	1–3	13
The Catalogs	4–6	14
Champion Eater	1–4	15
Choose Your Favorite Teacher	2–5	16
Citizens Of The Week	2–6	17
The Clown	1–4	18
Colored Tickets	3–6	19
Continuing Story	K–4	21
Cookie Jar	K–4	22
The Diary	5–6	23
Empire State Building	3–4	24
The Expectation	1–5	26
Extra Credit	4–6	27
Extra Recess—Class	3–6	28
Extra Recess—Individual	3–6	30
Fat Herbert	3–5	31

Flower In The Pot	1–3	32
Football	4–6	33
Free Homework Pass	4–6	35
Free Morning Or Afternoon	5–6	37
Good Start	K–1	38
Good Workers	K–3	39
Guts	3–6	40
The Handshake	2–4	42
The Happy Face	1–3	43
Help The Custodian	5–6	44
Homemade Ice Cream	4–6	45
Individual Activities	4–6	47
Individual Motivation Chart	3–5	48
Interest Centers	2–6	50
The Interesting Question	5–6	51
Intermittent Reinforcement	1–3	52
Keep Away	5–6	53
King And Queen For The Day	1–3	54
Kitchen Timer	2–5	55
Kits	4–6	56
The Lift	K–3	58
Love Notes	K–5	59
Lunch With The Principal	1–5	60
The Magic Touch	1–3	61
The Mail Carrier	K–3	62
Nonverbal Attention	1–3	64
The Number Right	2–6	65
The Nurse	K–3	66
Old Curiosity Cupboard	4–6	67
On Time	1–4	68
Our Friend	2–4	69
Partners	3–5	71
Peer Tutor	3–6	72
Peer Tutoring	3–6	73
Physical Education Reward	4–6	74
Picture A Day	1–3	75
Pitcher–Catcher	4–6	76

Pizza	4–6	77
Play Money	1–2	78
The Point Game	4–6	79
Principal's Helper	4–6	81
The Principal's Office	1–3	82
Proximity	K–3	83
The Punching Bag	2–6	84
Quiet Corners	3–6	85
Racetrack	3–6	86
Reading Train	1–2	88
Reading Worm	1–3	90
The Read-O-Meter	1–3	91
The Return Of The Toys	1–5	92
The Right Answer	2–5	94
Rita's Toys	2–4	95
Rockets To The Moon	4–6	96
School—A Pleasant Place To Work	4–6	98
School Phobia	K–3	100
Seat Of Honor	1–4	101
Seatwork	1–2	102
Seatwork Ticket	1–3	103
Shaping A Student	K–3	104
Showcase	5–6	105
The Silver Carpet	1–3	106
Special Carrier For The Day	K–3	107
Special Delivery	1–3	108
The Squeeze	1–3	109
Star On The Calendar	1–3	110
Surprise Bags	1–5	111
Tall Alex	5–6	112
Telephone Poles, Trees, And Houses	K–1	114
Thelma's Call	5–6	116
Time For Yourself	2–4	117
Token In The Can	1–3	118
The Touch	1–3	119
Two Drinks	3–5	120
Visit The Nurse	K–2	121

BONUS APPLICATIONS

Walking With The Principal	1–3	124
Win Your Name	2–4	125
Work At The Teacher's Desk	2–4	126
"X" On The Calendar	2–5	127
Yea Martin!	5–6	128

SUGGESTED READINGS   129

INDEXES

The Indexes that follow are designed to provide access to the 105 Applications from a variety of entry points. The Classified Index shows the title and the page number of each of the activities under one or more classifications of behavior patterns. In the Practical Applications section and in the Bonus section, each activity is labeled with an appropriate grade level and one descriptive behavioral classification. These labels are used in the Classified Index, and in most cases each activity is listed under one or more additional classifications. The Grade Level Index groups the activities according to the individual grade levels, from kindergarten through grade six.

Classified Index

xiv

ATTENTION SEEKING

Extra Credit, 27   Extra Recess—Individual, 30   Football, 33   Help The Custodian, 44   Peer Tutor, 72   Picture A Day, 75   Pizza, 77   Proximity, 83   The Return Of The Toys, 92   Thelma's Call, 116   Time For Yourself, 117   Visit The Nurse, 121   Walking With The Principal, 124   Yea Martin!, 128

DISRUPTIVE BEHAVIOR

Aquarium, 4   Bulletin Board Committee Row Game, 12   Citizens Of The Week, 17   Colored Tickets, 19   Extra Recess—Class, 28   Extra Recess—Individual, 30   Football, 33   Guts, 40   Help The Custodian, 44   Homemade Ice Cream, 45   Individual Activities, 47   Interest Centers, 50   Kitchen Timer, 55   Kits, 56   Love Notes, 59   Partners, 71   Peer Tutor, 72   Physical Education Reward, 74   Picture A Day, 75   Pitcher-Catcher, 76   Pizza, 77   The Point Game, 79   Principal's Helper, 81   Proximity, 83   Quiet Corners, 85   School—A Pleasant Place To Work, 98   Seatwork, 102   Special Delivery, 108   The Squeeze, 109   Thelma's Call, 116   Time For Yourself, 117   Two Drinks, 120   Walking With The Principal, 124   Work At The Teacher's Desk, 126   "X" On The Calendar, 127   Yea Martin!, 128

IMPROVING CLASS ATTITUDES

Befriending A Classmate, 7   Bulletin Board Committee Row Game, 12   Citizens Of The Week, 17   Continuing Story, 21   Cookie Jar, 22   Fat Herbert, 31   Free Morning Or Afternoon, 37   Good Start, 38   Guts, 40   Homemade Ice Cream, 45   Individual Motivation Chart, 48   The Interesting Question, 51   Keep Away, 53   Love Notes, 59   Our Friend, 69   Seatwork Ticket, 103   Showcase, 105   The Silver Carpet, 106   Work At The Teacher's Desk, 126   Yea Martin!, 128

IMPROVING MATHEMATICS SKILLS

The Buddies, 11   The Catalogs, 14   Empire State Building, 24   The Handshake, 42   The Happy Face, 43   Lunch With The Principal, 60   Peer Tutoring, 73   Token In The Can, 118   Two Drinks, 120

IMPROVING READING SKILLS

Beat Your Own Score, 5   Flower In The Pot, 32   Intermittent Reinforcement, 52   Lunch With The Principal, 60   Physical Education Reward, 74   Play Money, 78   Racetrack, 86   Reading Train,

88 Reading Train, 88 Reading Worm, 90 The Read-O-Meter, 91 Rita's Toys, 95 Seatwork Ticket, 103 Time For Yourself, 117

INADEQUATE ACADEMIC PERFORMANCE

After School Helper, 2 The Big Clap, 8 Breakfast In School, 10 The Buddies, 11 Bulletin Board Committee Row Game, 12 Carbon Paper, 13 The Catalogs, 14 Champion Eater, 15 Choose Your Favorite Teacher, 16 The Clown, 18 Colored Tickets, 19 Continuing Story, 21 Cookie Jar, 22 Empire State Building, 24 Flower In The Pot, 32 The Handshake, 42 The Happy Face, 43 Homemade Ice Cream, 45 Individual Motivation Chart, 48 The Interesting Question, 51 Keep Away, 53 King And Queen For The Day, 54 The Lift, 58 Lunch With The Principal, 60 The Magic Touch, 61 The Mail Carrier, 62 The Number Right, 65 Old Curiosity Cupboard, 67 Peer Tutoring, 73 Principal's Helper, 81 The Principal's Office, 82 The Read-O-Meter, 91 The Right Answer, 94 Rockets To The Moon, 96 Seat Of Honor, 101 The Squeeze, 109 Telephone Poles, Trees, And Houses, 114 The Touch, 119 Win Your Name, 125 Work At The Teacher's Desk, 126

INATTENTIVENESS

The Big Clap, 8 Bulletin Board Committee Row Game, 12 The Handshake, 42 The Mail Carrier, 62 Nonverbal Attention, 64 Old Curiosity Cupboard, 67 Physical Education Reward, 74 Play Money, 78 The Read-O-Meter, 91 The Return Of The Toys, 92 The Right Answer, 94 Rita's Toys, 95 School—A Pleasant Place To Work, 98 Seatwork, 102 Token In The Can, 118 The Touch, 119 Walking With The Principal, 124 Win Your Name, 125

INCOMPLETE CLASSWORK

After School Helper, 2 The Anecdote, 3 Breakfast In School, 10 The Clown, 18 Continuing Story, 21 Empire State Building, 24 Free Homework Pass, 35 Free Morning Or Afternoon, 37 The Interesting Question, 51 Intermittent Reinforcement, 52 Nonverbal Attention, 64 The Principal's Office, 82 The Read-O-Meter, 91 The Return Of The Toys, 92 Rita's Toys, 95 Shaping A Student, 104 Time For Yourself, 117 Walking With The Principal, 124 Win Your Name, 125

LEISURE TIME

Aquarium, 4 Extra Credit, 27 Interest Centers, 50 Kits, 56

MAINTAINING GOOD PERFORMANCE
The Anecdote, **3**   Cookie Jar, **22**   The Expectation, **26**   Free Morning Or Afternoon, **37**   Good Workers, **39**   The Punching Bag, **84**   Special Carrier For The Day, **107**

MOTOR SKILLS
Carbon Paper, **13**   Champion Eater, **15**

SELF-IMAGE
Befriending A Classmate, **7**   Champion Eater, **15**   The Clown, **18**   The Diary, **23**   Good Start, **38**   Individual Motivation Chart, **48**   Intermittent Reinforcement, **52**   Keep Away, **53**   Kits, **56**   The Lift, **58**   The Magic Touch, **61**   The Nurse, **66**   Racetrack, **86**   School Phobia, **99**   Seatwork, **102**   Tall Alex, **112**   Walking With The Principal, **124**   Win Your Name, **125**   Yea Martin!, **128**

SOCIAL SKILLS
Befriending A Classmate, **7**   Champion Eater, **15**   The Clown, **18**   The Diary, **23**   Fat Herbert, **31**   Guts, **40**   Individual Activities, **47**   The Nurse, **66**   Our Friend, **69**   Pitcher–Catcher, **76**   School Phobia, **99**   Showcase, **105**   Tall Alex, **112**   Visit The Nurse, **121**

TARDINESS AND ABSENTEEISM
The Bookshelf, **9**   On Time, **68**   School Phobia, **99**   Star On The Calendar, **110**   Surprise Bags, **111**

Grade Level Index

KINDERGARTEN

Continuing Story, 43   Cookie Jar, 44   Good Start, 58   Good Workers, 59   The Lift, 77   Love Notes, 78   The Mail Carrier, 81   The Nurse, 85   Proximity, 102   School Phobia, 117   Shaping A Student, 122   Special Carrier For The Day, 126   Telephone Poles, Trees, And Houses, 136   Visit The Nurse, 140

GRADE ONE

Aquarium, 28   Carbon Paper, 36   Champion Eater, 38   The Clown, 41   Continuing Story, 43   Cookie Jar, 44   The Expectation, 47   Flower In The Pot, 53   Good Start, 58   Good Workers, 59   The Happy Face, 62   Intermittent Reinforcement, 71   King And Queen For The Day, 73   The Lift, 77   Love Notes, 78   Lunch With The Principal, 79   The Magic Touch, 80   The Mail Carrier, 81   Nonverbal Attention, 83   The Nurse, 85   On Time, 87   Picture A Day, 94   Play Money, 97   The Principal's Office, 101   Proximity, 102   Reading Train, 107   Reading Worm, 109   The Read-O-Meter, 110   The Return Of The Toys, 111   School Phobia, 117   Seat Of Honor, 118   Seatwork, 119   Seatwork Ticket, 120   Shaping A Student, 122   The Silver Carpet, 124   Special Carrier For The Day, 126   Special Delivery, 127   The Squeeze, 128   Star On The Calendar, 129   Surprise Bags, 130   Token In The Can, 135   Telephone Poles, Trees, And Houses, 136   The Touch, 137   Visit The Nurse, 140   Walking With The Principal, 142

GRADE TWO

Aquarium, 28   The Big Clap, 31   Breakfast In School, 33   Carbon Paper, 36   Champion Eater, 38   Choose Your Favorite Teacher, 39   Citizens Of The Week, 40   The Clown, 41   Continuing Story, 43   Cookie Jar, 44   The Expectation, 47   Flower In The Pot, 53   Good Workers, 59   The Handshake, 61   The Happy Face, 62   Interest Centers, 69   Intermittent Reinforcement, 71   King and Queen For The Day, 73   Kitchen Timer, 75   The Lift, 77   Love Notes, 78   Lunch With The Principal, 79   The Magic Touch, 80   The Mail Carrier, 81   Nonverbal Attention, 83   The Number Right, 84   The Nurse, 85   On Time, 87   Our Friend, 88   Picture A Day, 94   Play Money, 97   The Principal's Office, 101   Proximity, 102   The Punching Bag, 103   Reading Train, 107   Reading Worm, 109   The Read-O-Meter, 110   The Return Of The Toys, 111   The Right Answer, 112   Rita's Toys, 113   School Phobia, 117   Seat Of

xvii

xviii

Honor, 118   Seatwork, 119   Seatwork Ticket, 120   Shaping A Student, 122   The Silver Carpet, 124   Special Carrier For The Day, 126   Special Delivery, 127   The Squeeze, 128   Star On The Calendar, 129   Surprise Bags, 130   Time For Yourself, 134   Token In The Can, 135   The Touch, 137   Visit The Nurse, 140   Walking With The Principal, 142   Win Your Name, 143   Work At The Teacher's Desk, 144   "X" On The Calendar, 145

GRADE THREE

Aquarium, 28   Beat Your Own Score, 29   The Big Clap, 31   The Bookshelf, 32   Breakfast In School, 33   The Buddies, 34   Carbon Paper, 36   Champion Eater, 38   Choose Your Favorite Teacher, 39   Citizens Of The Week, 40   The Clown, 41   Colored Tickets, 42   Continuing Story, 43   Cookie Jar, 44   Empire State Building, 46   The Expectation, 47   Extra Recess—Class, 50   Extra Recess—Individual, 51   Fat Herbert, 52   Flower In The Pot, 53   Good Workers, 59   Guts, 60   The Handshake, 61   The Happy Face, 62   Individual Motivation Chart, 68   Interest Centers, 69   Intermittent Reinforcement, 71   King And Queen For The Day, 73   Kitchen Timer, 75   The Lift, 77   Love Notes, 78   Lunch With The Principal, 79   The Magic Touch, 80   The Mail Carrier, 81   Nonverbal Attention, 83   The Number Right, 84   The Nurse, 85   On Time, 87   Our Friend, 88   Partners, 90   Peer Tutor, 91   Peer Tutoring, 92   Picture A Day, 94   The Principal's Office, 101   Proximity, 102   The Punching Bag, 103   Quiet Corners, 104   Racetrack, 105   Reading Worm, 109   The Read-O-Meter, 110   The Return Of The Toys, 111   The Right Answer, 112   Rita's Toys, 113   School Phobia, 117   Seat Of Honor, 118   Seatwork Ticket, 120   Shaping A Student, 122   The Silver Carpet, 124   Special Carrier For The Day, 126   Special Delivery, 127   The Squeeze, 128   Star On The Calendar, 129   Surprise Bags, 130   Time For Yourself, 134   Token In The Can, 135   The Touch, 137   Two Drinks, 139   Walking With The Principal, 142   Win Your Name, 143   Work At The Teacher's Desk, 144   "X" On The Calendar, 145

GRADE FOUR

The Anecdote, 27   Beat Your Own Score, 29   The Big Clap, 31   The Bookshelf, 32   Breakfast In School, 33   The Buddies, 34   Bulletin Board Committee Row Game, 35   The Catalogs, 37   Champion Eater, 38   Choose Your Favorite Teacher, 39   Citizens Of The Week, 40   The Clown, 41   Colored Tickets, 42   Continuing

Story, 43 Cookie Jar, 44 Empire State Building, 46 The Expectation, 47 Extra Credit, 49 Extra Recess—Class, 50 Extra Recess—Individual, 51 Fat Herbert, 52 Football, 54 Free Homework Pass, 55 Guts, 60 The Handshake, 61 Homemade Ice Cream, 65 Individual Activities, 66 Individual Motivation Chart, 68 Interest Centers, 69 Kitchen Timer, 75 Kits, 76 Love Notes, 78 Lunch With The Principal, 79 The Number Right, 84 Old Curiosity Cupboard, 86 On Time, 87 Our Friend, 88 Partners, 90 Peer Tutor, 91 Peer Tutoring, 92 Physical Education Reward, 93 Pitcher–Catcher, 95 Pizza, 96 The Point Game, 98 Principal's Helper, 100 The Punching Bag, 103 Quiet Corners, 104 Racetrack, 105 The Return Of The Toys, 111 The Right Answer, 112 Rita's Toys, 113 Rockets To The Moon, 114 School—A Pleasant Place To Work, 116 Seat Of Honor, 118 Surprise Bags, 130 Time For Yourself, 134 Two Drinks, 139 Win Your Name, 143 Work At The Teacher's Desk, 144 "X" On The Calendar, 145

GRADE FIVE

After School Helper, 26 The Anecdote, 27 Beat Your Own Score, 29 Befriending A Classmate, 30 The Big Clap, 31 The Bookshelf, 32 Breakfast In School, 33 The Buddies, 34 Bulletin Board Committee Row Game, 35 The Catalogs, 37 Choose Your Favorite Teacher, 39 Citizens Of The Week, 40 Colored Tickets, 42 The Diary, 45 The Expectation, 47 Extra Credit, 49 Extra Recess—Class, 50 Extra Recess—Individual, 51 Fat Herbert, 52 Football, 54 Free Homework Pass, 55 Free Morning Or Afternoon, 57 Guts, 60 Help The Custodian, 64 Homemade Ice Cream, 65 Individual Activities, 66 Individual Motivation Chart, 68 Interest Centers, 69 The Interesting Question, 70 Keep Away, 72 Kitchen Timer, 75 Kits, 76 Love Notes, 78 Lunch With The Principal, 79 The Number Right, 84 Old Curiosity Cupboard, 86 Partners, 90 Peer Tutor, 91 Peer Tutoring, 92 Physical Education Reward, 93 Pitcher–Catcher, 95 Pizza, 96 The Point Game, 98 Principal's Helper, 100 The Punching Bag, 103 Quiet Corners, 104 Racetrack, 105 The Return Of The Toys, 111 The Right Answer, 112 Rockets To The Moon, 114 School—A Pleasant Place To Work, 116 Showcase, 123 Surprise Bags, 130 Tall Alex, 131 Thelma's Call, 133 Two Drinks, 139 "X" On The Calendar, 145 Yea Martin!, 146

GRADE SIX

After School Helper, 26   The Anecdote, 27   Beat Your Own Score, 29   Befriending A Classmate, 30   The Bookshelf, 32   Breakfast In School, 33   The Buddies, 34   Bulletin Board Committee Row Game, 35   The Catalogs, 37   Citizens Of The Week, 40   Colored Tickets, 42   The Diary, 45   Extra Credit, 49   Extra Recess—Class, 50   Extra Recess—Individual, 51   Football, 54   Free Homework Pass, 55   Free Morning Or Afternoon, 57   Guts, 60   Help The Custodian, 64   Homemade Ice Cream, 65   Individual Activities, 66   Interest Centers, 69   The Interesting Question, 70   Keep Away, 72   Kits, 76   The Number Right, 84   Old Curiosity Cupboard, 86   Peer Tutor, 91   Peer Tutoring, 92   Physical Education Reward, 93   Pitcher–Catcher, 95   Pizza, 96   The Point Game, 98   Principal's Helper, 100   The Punching Bag, 103   Quiet Corners, 104   Racetrack, 105   Rockets To The Moon, 114   School—A Pleasant Place To Work, 116   Showcase, 123   Tall Alex, 131   Thelma's Call, 133   Yea Martin!, 146

Introduction

WHAT IS BEHAVIOR MODIFICATION?

Behavior modification is a systematic, positive way of changing human behavior. It operates on the premise that most behavior is learned. Therefore, new forms of behavior can be learned and substituted for ineffective ones. Behavior modification systems are designed to identify and utilize factors that can positively motivate children to learn new forms of behavior. These factors are called positive reinforcers. Reinforcers can "turn children on" and cause them to perform at higher cognitive, affective, and psychomotor levels in classrooms. Reinforcers can decrease children's tendencies to engage in negative or disruptive kinds of behavior.

Positive Reinforcement

The principle of positive reinforcement operates as follows:

1. If a teacher positively reinforces the desirable acts of a child in the classroom and ignores the undesirable ones, eventually the number of times that a child will perform undesirable acts will decrease as the desirable behavior increases.
2. If a teacher positively reinforces a child for work completed instead of focusing on incomplete work, the child's performance level will continue to increase.

The use of behavior modification in a classroom can motivate children in ways that cause them to be happier and to have better self-images. It can increase the quality of their production and reduce the frequency of disruptive acts. It can also increase teacher effectiveness with all students in the classroom and provide better instructional time, both qualitatively and quantitatively.

So that teachers, as well as others who work with children, can get ideas quickly for setting up behavior modification programs, this book has been prepared with this brief introductory explanation of behavior modification, followed by a total of one hundred five scenarios showing how behavior modification principles may be effectively applied in the classroom.

Positive Reinforcers

Positive reinforcers are at the heart of the programs of behavior modification. Without them the programs do not operate effectively. With them the programs can be most successful. Following is a list of factors teachers have found to be positively reinforcing in the production of desirable student behaviors.

Praise

Verbal praise is usually given to a child for doing what he or she is supposed to be doing—working quietly at a desk, answering questions appropriately, listening to and following directions. "That's a fine job, Johnnie," "You are really great. You are a real helper," "You make me very proud of you," "I like you because . . . ." are all examples of effective forms of verbal praise.

Written words of praise may also be used as reinforcers on a student's paper. Examples might be, "Excellent," "Wonderful," or "Very Good." Some children also enjoy "Snoopy is very happy with this paper," "You are improving," "This paper shows me that you are working very hard," or "I know that you will do even better next week."

Smile

A smile can be used when verbalization might interrupt a class. A smile coupled with verbal praise will provide a child with a double reinforcer. Attention of this nature, given frequently, can be very effective and requires a minimal amount of time and effort on the part of the teacher.

Nod or wink
A nod of the head, wink of the eye, thumbs up, the O.K. sign, and pointing an index finger signify social approval to the child. They can be used when verbalization might interrupt a class.

Symbols
The most common symbols that are used by teachers as positive reinforcers are happy faces, stars, and stickers. Children enjoy having the symbols on their papers and will work hard to earn them.

Proximity to a significant adult
When a teacher stands near a child during a lesson, a feeling of status or importance comes to the child, as well as a feeling of warmth. For greater emphasis, verbal praise can be given while the teacher is near by, if praise is appropriate.

Physical contact
Physical contact can give some children the feeling of social approval or the impression that someone cares for them. Examples of physical contact that appear to be positively reinforcing are a handshake, a gentle tap on the forehead with a magic wand or a finger, lifting a child up to show joy or improvement, and putting the palm of your hand on the child's head.

Food
Food is a positive reinforcer for most children, provided that the children have not become satiated with the particular type of food being offered to them. Cookies, lollipops, and ice cream appear to have great appeal to children.

Food works best as a positive reinforcer with deprived children who have had inadequate intakes of nourishment.

In hospital settings, food is used to modify behavior by giving children bits of food for successive approximations to a desired behavioral response. This practice is called the "shaping of behavior" and is an extremely effective way of teaching new behaviors.

Tokens or points

Tokens or points are given when children display proper types of behavior. They may be given to individuals or to groups of children. They acquire reinforcing properties when they enable a child to purchase items which he can take home or which may be used in school during recess or free time. A child may have to pay five tokens to use a microscope, three for a puzzle, two for a book, and so on. The number of tokens children might be expected to spend at various times is regulated according to what the teacher would like them to do with their spare time. Low priced items might be those the teacher wants a child to utilize, while higher priced items might be the ones the child wants to do and will work harder to earn. For example, a child might have to pay only two tokens for a book, but ten for a basketball. Some teachers substitute points for tokens.

Privileges

Instead of buying an item that can be used during leisure time, a child might earn the right to a privilege by amassing a number of points. Examples of some privileges which many children enjoy in schools are being first in line, being last in line, being the teacher's helper, sitting in a seat of honor, performing before the class, reading a story to a lower group, having a free morning to visit or work in any part of the building or with another class, tutoring another child, and having lunch with the principal.

Some teachers use one positive reinforcer, while others may use several in an attempt to produce change more rapidly. Some expend funds for positive reinforcers and others spend nothing with results that are often equally satisfactory. Of greatest significance, however, is the principle that the positive reinforcer be selected very carefully for each child.

Using Positive Reinforcers

The suggestions given below will help you implement a program of positive reinforcement. A basic principle to be followed, of course, is to try to change only one behavior at a time, thus improving the child's chance of succeeding.

- Positive reinforcers for a particular child can be determined by observing the child to see what he or she likes, or by simply asking the child to state a preference from among an array of alternatives. Giving a child choices or alternatives is better than presenting the child with only one choice, because the item chosen may not be a positive reinforcer for that child. What is a positive reinforcer to one child may not be a positive reinforcer to another. One may like cookies or ice cream, another may not.

- When using praise as a positive reinforcer, the praise should be varied, spontaneous, and delivered frequently, particularly when the system is being initiated. Praise should be genuine and full of enthusiasm. Praising children for correct work will be more effective than concentrating on the number of wrong answers given.

- The hierarchy for using positive reinforcers should start with praise. If praise does not work, the teacher should move toward a point or token system. If the latter does not work, a time-out zone should be established, particularly for students with highly disruptive behavior patterns. A student in a time-out zone is not permitted to earn points. The loss of the opportunity to earn points usually helps to change the student's behavior, especially when other students are being given many opportunities for earning points. Other children can often be given extra points for ignoring a disruptive child's behavior. When the disruptive child no longer has an active audience to reinforce the negative behaviors, these patterns often change to more acceptable ones.

- When initiating a point system, provide many opportunities for children to earn points or positive reinforcers. If the earning power is too slow or beyond the child's sense of possibility, the system will not work. The system should be arranged to help the child earn points for even the slightest amount of improvement. At times, you may have to invent ways to give a child extra or bonus points, earning power, or encouragement.
- It is important for a child to see a visual display or illustration depicting his progress, daily, hourly, or at significant intervals of minutes determined by the needs of the individual child. The visual display encourages the child to evaluate his or her progress frequently, which in turn enhances the pressure to improve the behavior patterns.

One of the most important points to remember is to dispense the positive reinforcer immediately. It is much more effective to tell a child that he or she is doing well while the activity is occurring than to wait until another activity has intruded.

Being an enthusiastic teacher helps create enthusiastic learners.

THE CONTRACT SYSTEM

Oral or written contracts often make use of positive reinforcers. A contract can be made with children, individually or as a group, letting them know that they can earn items or privileges for their free time, based upon proper classroom behavior and performance. In some contractual relationships children may work for only one kind of positive reinforcer. On other occasions, they may be permitted to work for a variety of reinforcers.

When using a written contract, it is important that both the child and all significant adults sign the contract. The signatures appear to make the contract more important for the child. Written contracts, in general, appear to be more binding than oral one.

To determine the method of reinforcement for the contract, the following procedures can be used:

Ask the child or the class to list a number of items or privileges which they would like to have, or for which they would be willing to work.

Have the child or the class rank those items or privileges in order of preference. If a child or a class will work for only one positive reinforcer, that item probably has the greatest reinforcing value to those pupils. Examples of such reinforcers might be extra recess time or getting to play a certain game. Each of these often causes a child or class to work harder and for a longer period of time. It is important to use the reinforcer that is most stimulating to your class.

Assign a point value to each item or privilege if a number of positive reinforcers are going to be used as part of a contract.

Give the greatest number of points to the positive reinforcer that appears to be of most value to the child or the class.

Once the positive reinforcers have been determined, the teacher can then write up the contract with the child or children. As soon as the contract is written and signed, the child or children start executing it.

STARTING A PROGRAM OF BEHAVIOR MODIFICATION

Behavior modification programs need not be complicated. The following is a simple procedure for instituting a program of behavior modification in a classroom.

Observe and identify the most critical behavior that is in need of change. For example, Bobby continually talks out.

Record the frequency of the behavior during a given block of time, such as the first fifteen minutes out of each hour in school. Example: count the number of times that Bobby talks out from 9:00 to 9:15 a.m., 10:00 to 10:15 a.m., etc. This count establishes the "baseline."

Write on a piece of paper in positive terms the behavior you desire from Bobby. Example: "I want Bobby to work quietly."

Plan a program to produce change through the use of a positive reinforcer. Praise is a positive reinforcer for most children. Remember that children thrive on reinforcement. If a teacher positively reinforces the desirable acts of children in a classroom and ignores the undesirable ones, eventually the number of times a child will perform undesirable acts will decrease as the desirable behavior increases in frequency.

Institute the plan. For example: when Bobby is working quietly, praise him often by expressions such as, "I like the quiet way Bobby is working." Refrain from giving Bobby attention when he is talking out.

Evaluate the plan to determine if change is taking place. Record the frequency of the undesirable behavior, as was previously done. Compare both sets of records. If the frequency of the undesirable behavior is decreasing, continue using the positive reinforcer. If not, look for another factor that might be positively reinforcing and try it.

ONE HUNDRED PRACTICAL APPLICATIONS

Grades 5-6 / Incomplete Classwork

After School Helper

Situation
Helen is doing poor school work and seldom finishes it. Materials have been carefully prescribed to match her success level. Despite the teacher's efforts, Helen is disinterested in her work and is generally unhappy.

Strategy
1. Talk to Helen. Tell her what work you expect her to complete for the day.
2. Make a contract giving Helen a point for each completed assignment, and a bonus point for any lengthy one. Keep assignments short to insure success.
3. Let Helen know that she can be an after school helper when she has earned 10 points.
4. For an additional bonus, give Helen and her classmates 15 minutes of extra recess each time that she has accumulated 25 points.

Rationale
1. To ask Helen why she has not completed her assignments often does little to change her behavior pattern.
2. It is better to work out a plan of incentives that will cause her to complete the assigned tasks.
3. Having Helen serve as an after school helper may make her feel good about the extra position of status.
4. This strategy provides the teacher with an opportunity to counsel Helen on an individual basis while alone with her after school.

Grades 4-6 / Incomplete Classwork

The Anecdote

Situation
You want to improve student work habits. You want the students to refrain from wasting time and to complete all of the assigned work within a given time.

Strategy
1. Be prepared to tell the students an anecdote that will be of interest to them. Plan on doing it at the end of the morning or afternoon session.
2. At the beginning of the morning session in a soft voice say something such as, "How many of you have heard about the City of Children where the mayor was 12 years old?
   "When we complete our work this morning, I shall tell you about it."
3. Throughout the morning or afternoon periodically say, "I certainly hope we have time to discuss the City of Children today."

Rationale
1. The opportunity to hear the anecdote can serve to reinforce completing tasks on time.
2. Curiosity is used in this instance as an affective catalyst to motivate children.

Grades 1-3 / Disruptive Behavior

Aquarium

Situation
Shari often completes her work sooner than the other students. Sometimes you give her more work to do, but she seems to resent the extra work. She is somewhat disruptive when she has too much leisure time. Shari appears to enjoy the aquarium in your room.

Strategy
1. Put Shari in charge of the aquarium, while other children are permitted to observe the fish or feed them.
2. Let Shari keep a chart or daily record of children who have visited the aquarium.

Rationale
1. Many children are fascinated by an aquarium. Merely watching the fish has a hypnotic soothing effect upon them.
2. Shari's interest in an aquarium coupled with a position of status can enhance her self-image and channel Shari's behavior into more acceptable patterns.
3. Too often teachers will give children more work if they finish assignments early. Children should be rewarded, not punished, for being productive.

Grades 3-6 / *Improving Reading Skills*

Beat Your Own Score

Situation

Ted is an upper grade student. He reads on a first grade level. He has had difficulty with the written word and has had previous failures in reading. He has developed a distaste toward reading. To lessen his frustrations with the written page you would like Ted to develop a sight vocabulary of the Dolch 220 most common words in the English Language. You plan to use a phonics approach with Ted after he has mastered a basic sight vocabulary.

Strategy

1. Make a matrix with five-point intervals from 0 to 220 along the left side with ten columns across the top representing the ten months of school.
2. Explain to Ted that you have made a chart on which a monthly record will be kept of the number of words he can recognize.
3. Test Ted to see how many words he can recognize from the Dolch 220 list and mark that number in the first column on his chart.
4. Make a contract with Ted which permits him to choose a free hour of activities each time he beats his own score.
5. Use various games, flash cards, a language master, parents, peer helpers and other resources available to teach more ff the 220 words. You could review previously learned words and add five words daily.
6. Each month retest Ted to see how many of the Dolch words he can recognize.
7. Enter that number on his chart.
8. If Ted beats his own score, reinforce him according to the contract.
9. Continue the same practice each month that Ted beats his own score until he masters the 220 words.

Rationale
1. Children are often afraid to compete with their peers for fear of failure and possible ridicule.
2. Children are usually less anxious when competing with themselves, against their own previous records.
3. Setting up a chart for a child gives a visual indication of progress being made.
4. Dividing the chart into small segments for each five words is better than making divisions for ten, fifteen, or twenty words because smaller amounts of improvements appear to be greater in the eyes of students.

Grades 5-6 / Improving Class Attitudes

Befriending A Classmate

Situation
Ralph does not get along with the children in his class. They continually pick on him and go out of their way to be nasty to him. Their nastiness sets him off. One day when tapped on the head by an unknown student, he became so angry that he kicked in the door of a cupboard under a counter in the room. You want to improve the class's attitude toward Ralph and to lessen his outbursts.

Strategy
1. When Ralph is not in the room talk frankly with the children about Ralph's behavior and the things they do not like.
2. Ask them why they feel that Ralph is behaving in the manner that he does and what brings on his outbursts.
3. After the children have expressed their negativeness toward Ralph, ask them how he can be helped so that the number of emotional outbursts can be reduced.
4. Tell the children that if they befriend Ralph, help him with his work, and keep him from having any emotional outbursts for four and one half days, they may have extra privileges on the fifth day at the noon recess. (One of the favorite privileges is an extra half hour of recess.)
5. Find out from the children who will initially try to befriend Ralph and what steps will be taken to improve Ralph's behavior. When successful, give the children an extra amount of recess as promised.

Rationale
1. Having the students discuss Ralph's behavior helps to give them insight into their own behavior.
2. They soon learn that Ralph's behavior can be changed when they modify their own behavior toward him. This is a valuable lesson in interpersonal relations.

Grades 2-5 / Inattentiveness

The Big Clap

Situation
George is inattentive in English classes and consequently does not know the right place in the book or gives the wrong answer. You want to improve his attention span as well as his classroom performance.

Strategy
1. Ask George a question that you know he can answer.
2. A few minutes later, ask George another question that he can answer.
3. Repeat the process shortly thereafter.
4. Say to the class, "Wasn't that great. George knew the answer to three of my questions. Let's all give George a big clap. He is really working today."
5. Clap for George on other occasions, as the clapping may reinforce his behavior.
6. A variation of the same thing is to ask the class to give George a silent clap. (This can be used when the noise might disturb another group or class working nearby.) A silent clap is done by striking the index finger against the palm of the opposite hand.

Rationale
1. Peer approval may be a factor in motivating George to be more attentive and should be used positively and readily.
2. A silent clap is particularly effective when noise could be distracting.

Grades 3-6 / Tardiness And Absenteeism

The Bookshelf

Situation
Adela is continually late for school. She uses a variety of excuses for being tardy. You would like her to come to school on time.

Strategy
1. Give Adela a job that she can complete in the classroom before the rest of the children come into the room.
2. Make sure that she likes the job and feels that she is doing you a real service in performing it.
3. Praise her for the work she is doing.
4. Examples of tasks that might be done by Adela are putting books on a bookshelf or straightening out a bookshelf or cupboard.
5. You can disarrange your books purposely each night so youngsters like Adela can feel they are making an important contribution to your classroom.

Rationale
1. This strategy makes the child feel that she is needed. It helps to give her status and to build up her self-esteem.
2. It also gives Adela a good reason for coming to school on time.

Grades 2-6 / Inadequate Academic Performance

Breakfast In School

Situation
You are not satisfied with the performance of your class on several academic projects. You want to motivate the children to do better work on future projects.

Strategy
1. Try breakfast in school as a positive reinforcer.
2. Set the total number of points needed to have breakfast in school at fifty.
3. Use five points a day for the class as the highest number for the best behavior, four for good behavior, three for fair behavior, and zero for poor behavior.
4. At the end of each day add the points for that day to the accumulated total.
5. When fifty points have been earned by the class, tell the children that they have earned the privilege of having breakfast in school.
6. Room mothers and cafeteria workers can help in making breakfast. If a cafeteria is not available, use hot plates in the regular classroom.
7. Allow the children to plan the menu.
8. The principal or a significant adult can be invited to show approval for the class's activity.
9. Breakfast in school can also cultivate the concept that school can be a pleasant place for children to work.

Rationale
1. Innovative teachers continually search for a variety of unique privileges that can be used successfully to enhance student attitudes and performance.
2. An extra privilege, such as breakfast in school, can be motivation to improve classroom performance.
3. This strategy can also present an opportunity for students to display skills other than academic.

Grades 3-6 / Improving Mathematics Skills

The Buddies

Situation
You have a group of children who do not know their number facts. You would like these children to gain mastery of them.

Strategy
1. Have the children in the class who know their facts serve as tutors.
2. Tell the tutors that as soon as a tutoree has mastered the facts a special privilege will be provided for the tutor and his or her partner.
3. Explore with the children privileges that they would like to earn.
4. Grant the tutor and partner the special privilege upon mastery of the facts.

Rationale
1. This technique teaches children to work cooperatively.
2. It encourages student ingenuity, particularly if the tutor is asked to invent a method of teaching his or her partner.
3. The tutor is given the opportunity to reinforce a knowledge of the number facts and sometimes profits even more than the one being tutored.

Grades 4-6 / Disruptive Behavior

Bulletin Board Committee Row Game

Situation
You have an aggressive class of boys who continually act up and thrive on competition. They are not performing as well as you would like. Poor student attention and concentration, as well as hyperactivity, are detrimental to the class.

Strategy
1. Play the row game which enables the team with the highest number of points for the week to design and decorate one of the class bulletin boards. Choose a leader for each row and make that person the captain.
2. Award points each hour for good behavior. Give the row with the best behavior five points. Give the next, four points, and others three, two, and one accordingly.
3. Keep a daily and weekly cumulative total.
4. Give the runner-up another type of privilege.
5. Repeat this process weekly.
6. If a boy is constantly preventing a row from winning, switch him to another row.
7. If someone who usually engages in undesirable behavior helps his team to win, his exceptional effort can be praised in front of the class. This may produce a dramatic change in the particular boy's behavior.

Rationale
1. The competitive nature of children often can be channeled into productive efforts.
2. Children like to decorate bulletin boards. Decorating allows for freedom of movement on their part. The student can work with his hands and it gives him a feeling of accomplishment.
3. Although the bulletin board could be more attractive if the teacher did the work, it is a learning experience for children to complete bulletin boards on their own.

Grades 1-3 / Inadequate Academic Performance

Carbon Paper

Situation
You are concerned with your students' handwriting. Some of the students are not writing as legibly as they might.

Strategy
1. Have your school secretary or the central business office personnel save used carbon paper for your use. There is usually plenty available from budget or requisition slips.
2. Give the students in your class a carbon paper as well as an extra sheet of paper whenever you would like them to produce a good handwriting paper.
3. Tell them that the duplicate copy will be displayed in an important part of the building, such as the area outside the principal's office, main lobby, or cafeteria.

Rationale
1. The changing of routine procedures can have a positive effect on the handwriting of the children.
2. Since children seldom use carbon paper, this technique can have a desirable result.

Grades 4-6 / Improving Mathematics Skills

The Catalogs

Situation
You have children in the classroom who do not know their number combinations. You want to motivate them to learn the combinations.

Strategy
1. Say to the children, "When you learn your number combinations, such as addition facts, I will give you some budget coupons and some publishers' catalogs. You will be permitted to write orders for one hundred dollars' worth of items from the catalogs; as I do for the principal. You may not order more than one hundred dollars' worth of materials, but you can order less if you wish."
2. When the particular number facts have been learned, let the child peruse the catalogs and start writing orders.

Rationale
1. This technique encourages the children to learn their number combinations and to participate in the privilege that is being offered.
2. It gives the child further experience in the use of the combinations in practical situations.
3. Most catalogs fascinate children and maintain their interest. Make sure you have a good selection.
4. This activity also provides valuable experience in addition and budgeting.

Grades 1-4 / Inadequate Academic Performance

Champion Eater

Situation
Delbert is a student with multiple problems. He has poor psychomotor skills, cognitive skills, and social skills.

Strategy
At the lunch table the teacher, principal, or counselor can sit next to Delbert and make positive remarks about his eating habits, such as, "Delbert is the champion eater" or "Delbert has terrific manners."

Rationale
1. Teachers sometimes indicate there is little they can find to positively praise in a child who does not perform well academically and socially.
2. This is an instance where the child can be praised for eating well, eating neatly, or practicing good eating habits.
3. Try to find something worthy of praise about each child.

Grades 2-5 / Inadequate Academic Performance

Choose Your Favorite Teacher

Situation
Margie is not reaching the goals you set for her. She is producing average work, but you are convinced Margie has the ability to achieve at a higher level.

Strategy
1. Let Margie indicate who her favorite teacher might be.
2. For a set number of points, permit Margie to visit her favorite teacher.
3. If Margie is older than the youngsters in the class she visits, then she could be a student tutor, read to the children, or lead the class in some kind of physical exercise.
4. If Margie is younger than most of the students in the class visited, a chosen student could play a game with her or teach her something that she might want to learn.

Rationale
1. Often a break in the routine makes children more productive after returning to their own classrooms.
2. It is egocentric and often unrealistic to think that your student's favorite teacher is YOU and she doesn't care for other teachers in the building.
3. Possibly the teacher that Margie chooses could become the supportive counselor that Margie may need to encourage her to achieve in your classroom.

Grades 2-6 / Disruptive Behavior

Citizens Of The Week

Situation
You want to improve the general behavior of your class. You want your children to think positively in terms of good behavior.

Strategy
1. With suggestions from the children make a list of characteristics that a "good citizen" should possess. Put the list on a chart that is on display in the classroom at all times.
2. Make another chart on which the names of the children are listed on the left side of the chart, from the top to the bottom. Divide the rest of the space on the chart into squares with Fridays throughout the year listed across the top of the chart.
3. On Fridays have the children nominate each other for the title of "Citizen of the Week," requiring them to prove why the nominee should be considered as a "Citizen of the Week." Have the children justify their nominations in terms of good deeds that have been performed, as well as the characteristics that have been previously set up in chart form.
4. Have the "Citizen of the Week" put a star in the block for the week on the chart which was made for this purpose. Encourage the children to earn many stars.

Rationale
1. In determining "Citizens of the Week," the class must make value judgments to determine the characteristics of a good citizen.
2. It also helps the students to continually evaluate their own behavior.
3. This technique also helps students to look for the good in others and to reinforce it.

Grades 1-4 / Inadequate Academic Performance

The Clown

Situation
Janell is a girl who has many emotional outbursts which prevent her from completing her assigned work. She gets angry quite often. You want to lessen the number of emotional outbursts and have her complete more of her assigned tasks.

Strategy
1. Purchase a plastic clown that springs back into place when you punch it. Put the clown in the back of the room.
2. Explain to the class that the clown can be loved or hit by children who complete their assignments.
3. Put Janell on a contract involving four time blocks in the morning session of the school.
4. At first, it may be necessary to use short blocks of time. These may be gradually lengthened.
5. Permit her to earn one point in each of those time blocks for work completed.
6. On days that she has earned four points let her give the clown four good punches. Eventually encourage her to change some of the punches to hugs.
7. Provide an alternative privilege that Janell can attain for earning only three points, perhaps the privilege of being first or last in line when it is time to go to the lunchroom to eat.

Rationale
1. The use of a clown is a good way of motivating a child to complete the assigned work.
2. It is better for Janell to hit a clown than to hit other children.

Grades 3-6 / Inadequate Academic Performance

Colored Tickets

Situation
Your class is not as productive as you would like it to be. Unnecessary talking and fooling around seem to minimize class productivity.

Strategy
1. Discuss your concern with the class and explain your plan for alleviating the situation.
2. Use five or six colors of construction paper to cut out 3" × 5" blank tickets, and disperse them in different key areas throughout the classroom.
3. Ring a bell approximately three or four times per hour at regular intervals. This will be the signal for the children to monitor their own behavior. If they are doing a task (working or listening at the time you ring the bell), they may take a ticket.
4. When the class accumulates a set number of tickets it should be given free reading time, extra recess time, or whatever it considers to be reinforcing.
5. Keep a running account of tickets accumulated on a monthly calendar so there can be a long range reinforcer.
6. The long range reinforcer should be particularly enticing to give the students some extra incentive to achieve the required number of points.

   For example: 200 points could purchase 10 minutes of extra recess, while 2,000 points could purchase the privilege of playing a game in the gymnasium against another class.

7. Another example might be to arrange to bring a parent or other visitor to the classroom with an interesting presentation. A class trip might also be taken.

Rationale
1. Students function best on an incentive system. Employees would not work as hard if their pay was decreased or eliminated. Children, in particular, cannot wait too long for their rewards as most of them live for the immediate future. Therefore, short term reinforcement is important. It is naive to think that a student learns because he will get a better job years from now.
2. A long range reward, such as going on a class trip in two months for points accrued, is usually more effective when it is coupled with a short term reinforcer.
3. A group ticket system may also be instrumental in encouraging the students who have not performed to work harder to gain peer approval and privileges.

Grades K-4 / Improving Class Attitudes

Continuing Story

Situation
You want to improve students' work habits in general and get pupils to complete all assignments for the morning or afternoon.

Strategy
1. Start reading a story that is of high interest value to children.
2. Stop at a significant part.
3. Tell the children that you will read more at the end of the next day if all work is completed on time.
4. At significant times in the morning praise the children for work accomplished and say, "I certainly hope that we have time for more of that story today."

Rationale
"The Continuing Story" heightens student curiosity to learn about the next episode which causes them to increase performance. This technique is sometimes called "reinforcer sampling" as it involves giving the person a sample of what is available before working for the rest of it.

Grades K-4 / Maintaining Good Performance

Cookie Jar

Situation
Robert has started to show some improvement in his work. You want Robert to continue to improve.

Strategy
1. Have the principal bring a cookie jar, filled with cookies, into the classroom.
2. Have him give the cookie jar to Robert and tell him to treat the class by giving each child a cookie.
3. Have the principal tell the class that the treat is being given because Robert has shown such fine improvement.
4. If there is a chance for other treats, the children in the class will encourage Robert to continue to improve.
5. The cookies can be obtained from a left-over function of the PTA.

Rationale
1. In the current situation the strategy of using a principal to praise Robert and dispense cookies was instrumental in improving Robert's peer group status, as well as his academic performance.
2. Food can be an effective reinforcer. Using food to reinforce the class tends to cause the students to have a better feeling toward Robert.
3. Peer group influences can also be used to help increase or maintain a student's level of performance.

Grades 5-6 / Social Skills

The Diary

Situation
There is poor social interaction among the students in your class. You want to improve the situation.

Strategy
1. Give each child a notebook for recording his or her feelings, concerns, and questions at the end of each school day, and call it a diary.
2. Keep a diary yourself.
3. Use the following rules with the diaries:
   a. All diaries should remain on the teacher's desk.
   b. The students may not look at each other's diaries.
   c. The teacher should read the student's diaries and write answers to their questions, or make comments in the diary.
   d. The students may read the teacher's diary in which are expressed the feelings about the school day.
4. The teacher should give the class considerable verbal praise for conveying their feelings honestly.

   Example: "It makes me happy and proud to be the teacher of a class that is so honest."

5. The individual names of students should not be mentioned in the teacher's diary. Individual diaries should be locked up at night to maintain confidentiality.

Rationale
1. The use of diaries helps the teacher to monitor the social structure of the classroom and to make necessary changes as the need arises.
2. Written aggression is more acceptable than physical aggression in the classroom. Both forms of aggression may be reduced if the teacher uses this technique.

Grades 3-4 / Improving Mathematics Skills

Empire State Building

Situation
Selma is having difficulty with math. She is not completing her assignments.

Strategy
1. Lessen the difficulty of the assignments so that Selma can experience success.
2. Draw on oaktag a large sketch of the Empire State Building with 100 floors.
3. Make twenty intervals — one for every five floors.
4. Make an elevator that can be moved from the first to the hundredth floor.
5. As Selma completes each math assignment have her move up five floors.
6. This chart need not be displayed for the class. It can remain private between the teacher and Selma.
7. A reinforcer can be worked out between Selma and the teacher, when the elevator reaches the top floor.

Rationale
1. This method gives Selma an opportunity to monitor her own progress.
2. Jumping five floors at a time is gratifying and motivates Selma to seek further accomplishment with her elevator.
3. Her elevator can only go upward. Selma cannot lose.
4. Success breeds success. Continued reinforcement with a reward for tasks completed provides both an intrinsic and extrinsic reward for the student.

EMPIRE STATE BUILDING

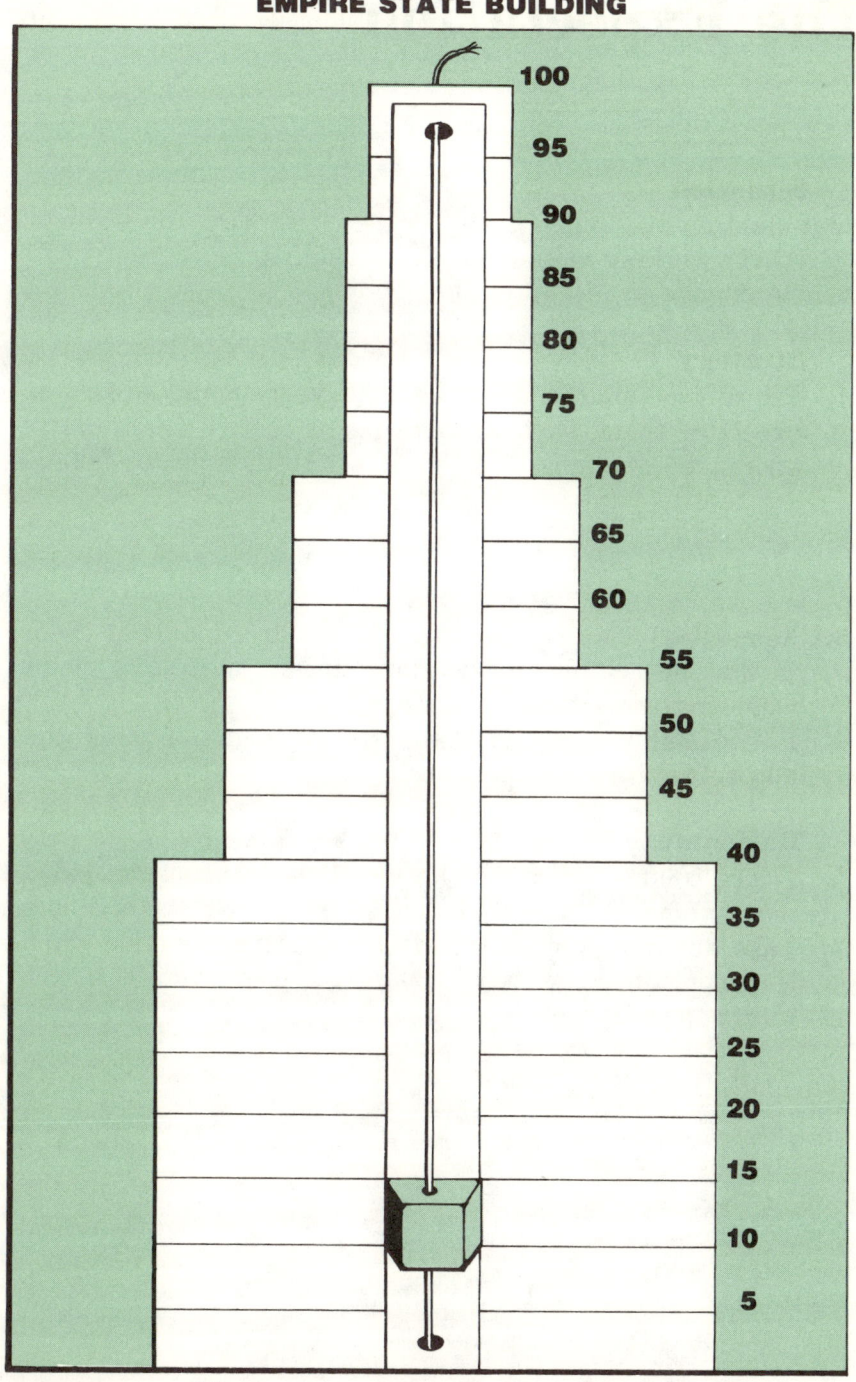

25

Elevator can move up and down on string.

Grades 1-5 / Maintaining Good Performance

The Expectation

Situation
Your children are working well in the classroom. You want to keep them working well. You do not want to encourage children to engage in disruptive behavior.

Strategy
1. Praise the children *often* when they are doing what you expect of them, such as working at their desks quietly, answering quetions in an appropriate manner, or listening to directions and following them.
2. Use words of praise such as, "You really make me proud of you." "You are doing a fine job." "I am so glad that you are in my room." "I like you."
3. Remember when you are praising children, smile at them so that they know that you are sincere and really mean what you are saying.
4. Praise children many, many times during each of the hours that they are in school.

Rationale
1. Praise coupled with a smile is a fine, inexpensive, effective reinforcer.
2. Take advantage of the children's positive behavior when the opportunity exists. "An ounce of prevention is better than a pound of cure."

Grades 4-6 / Attention Seeking

Extra Credit

Situation
Mario completes his work early and is continually seeking your attention for things to do.

Strategy
1. Have a box in the room marked "Extra Credit."
2. Let the students who finish their assignments early work on a project or paper of their choice. A list of alternatives may be provided for those who cannot decide what to do.
3. Have students place their completed assignments in the "Extra Credit" box.
4. Give students the opportunity to improve their grade with the extra credit work.
5. Extra credit can only be used to improve a grade.

Rationale
Teachers seem to be continually looking for ways to keep students constructively busy when they finish their work early. This provides the students with several alternatives which lead to greater academic productivity.
1. This technique helps the students to use time wisely and manage their affairs. The students can develop independence through choices and alternatives.
2. Children can develop their creative talent if they so desire. Some may elect to work on arts and crafts projects for their extra credit.

Grades 3-6 / Disruptive Behavior

Extra Recess — Class

Situation
The children in your class continually get out of their seats, run around the room and cause disruptions. You want your class to spend more time in productive activities.

Strategy
1. Have an open discussion with the children in your class concerning their behavior.
2. Tell the children that they can earn extra recess time for remaining in their seats and working.
3. Let them know that for every thirty minutes of proper behavior they can earn five points. When they earn a total of thirty points they can have fifteen additional minutes of recess.
4. Explain further that for every ten points they earn over thirty points in a given day they can have a bonus of an extra five minutes of recess.
5. Mark on the chalkboard in an area that the children can see the following numbers: 5, 10, 15, 20, 25, 30, 35, 40.
6. Circle each five points as the class progresses toward its goal of thirty points.
7. Praise the children each time they earn five points, and ask them how they would like to use the extra fifteen minutes of recess when it has been earned.
8. Give the children fifteen minutes of recess when they have reached their goal of thirty points.
9. Give the children additional recess near the closing of each school day during which sufficient bonus points have been earned.

Rationale
1. Extra recess time is often a strong reinforcer for both boys and girls. Consequently it can be used quite effectively to shape or modify student behavior.

2. Praising children and circling each five-point interval toward their goal helps to further motivate students to reach their final goal.
3. Circling each five-point interval also gives students a visual indication of how close they are to attaining their goal. As they come nearer to the thirty-point goal, they often try harder to contain themselves in order to earn extra recess time.
4. Extra recess can also help students to release excessive energies.

Grades 3-6 / Disruptive Behavior

Extra Recess — Individual

Situation
Max's general behavior is disruptive. He calls out in class, annoys his peers, and sometimes hits them.

Strategy
1. Say, "The whole class will get ten minutes of extra recess if Max doesn't fight."
2. Reinforce the class as promised on the first day that Max doesn't fight.
3. Praise Max for achieving this goal.
4. Have the class thank Max with applause, if appropriate, for the extra recess they will now have.
5. Provide an additional reinforcer if Max doesn't fight for one full week.

Rationale
1. In the situation Max has been motivated to refrain from fighting.
2. Peer group praise can often be used effectively to change a child's behavior. By placing a premium on not fighting, fewer skirmishes are triggered by minor incidents.
3. Working to change one kind of behavior at a time can often produce unexpected dividends for the teacher as a child's other behavior attitudes have a tendency to become more positive.
4. Giving a student additional attention may help him to achieve greater satisfaction in social situations and lessen his desire to fight.

Grades 3-5 / Improving Class Attitudes

Fat Herbert

Situation
Herbert is obese. He is out of place with his peers and consequently is not being accepted by them. You want Herbert to gain acceptance.

Strategy
1. In front of the class say, "I certainly like Herbert. He is so tall and strong. I can really use him to help me with the big jobs in the classroom."
2. Assign a job to Herbert. Tell him that he can select three "friends" from the class to help him.
3. On the next task Herbert can have the option of selecting the same three friends or others.
4. As he continues to perform tasks he should be encouraged to select other students to broaden his circle of friendships.

Rationale
1. The teacher can often be instrumental in having a class accept a student by showing that the teacher accepts him and considers his difference to be an asset.
2. Friendship can be created or enhanced by making a student like Herbert the person who selects others to assist him in the performance of tasks for the teacher.
3. Students soon realize that it is important for them to befriend Herbert if they are to be selected to perform tasks in the classroom.

Grades 1-3 / Improving Reading Skills

Flower In The Pot

Situation
Your children are having difficulty recognizing words. You want to increase the number of words the children can instantly recognize and know their meanings.

Strategy
1. Tell the children that you are starting a new flower bulletin board that will grow as recognition of words increases and learning becomes evident.
2. Tack a paper flower pot on the bulletin board for each child in the room.
3. When a child learns five new words, write the words and the child's name on a flower pot. The child can "grow" a flower by learning new words.
4. When the child learns five more words, put a paper stem in the flower pot. Write the five new words on it.
5. Follow a similar process to add leaves and petals.
6. When the flower has been completed, permit the child to take all parts off the bulletin board, reassemble and paste them on a piece of construction paper. Let the child take it home as a flower picture.

Rationale
1. The bulletin board provides each child with a visual representation of the number of words learned.
2. The teacher has an interesting, developing bulletin board, while at the same time children are being motivated to learn.
3. Adding parts to the flower continually, positively reinforces the children to learn more words.
4. Being able to take the flower picture home serves as an additional reinforcer and gives the parents a chance to add further reinforcing.

Grades 4-6 / Disruptive Behavior

Football

Situation
The class is disruptive and difficult to control. The boys seem to be responsible for most of the poor behavior. You would like to change their negative behavior. You are well aware of the fact that the boys enjoy football and you are going to use this vehicle to direct their aggressive energies into more constructive channels.

Strategy
1. Draw a football field on the chalkboard, marking off every ten yards.
2. Make an oaktag football with a circle of masking tape on the back of it.
3. Place it on the 20-yard line.
4. Tell the children they are going to play a football game with the following rules:
   a. For each 15 minutes of satisfactory classroom behavior, the teacher will advance the football 5 yards toward the goal line.
   b. When a touchdown is scored, the class will be given the privilege of playing an actual game of touch football.
5. Other game options may be provided for students who do not care to participate in football.

Rationale
1. The football game capitalizes upon the students' interest in sports and game-like activities.
2. The simulated game is the vehicle that is instrumental in enabling the students to participate in actual games.
3. It gives the students a visual picture of the progress they are making toward their goal.
4. The simulated game is also designed with 16 advances that will take four or more hours before a touchdown can

be scored, making it possible for the students to play a new game each day.
5. If the children don't quite make a touchdown on a given day, they can continue the next day where they left off, still giving the students a chance to win.
6. The football redirects excessive energy into positive channels.

Grades 4-6 / Incomplete Classwork

Free Homework Pass

Situation

Toshi is a girl who is involved in many activities after school. Some have to do with organizations such as Girl Scouts, Little League, and her church. On other occasions she is busy taking part in family activities. As a result of her many activities, she often arrives for school without having the homework assignments completed. You want her to complete her homework and hand it in on time.

Strategy

1. Tell your class that any child who has his or her homework done correctly and turned in on time for five nights can earn a "free homework pass" that can be used on any afternoon or night, particularly when the family has planned activities or when there is a Little League game. It is a form or a contract that is contingent upon performance.
2. Give the children at least five or ten minutes each day to start their homework so they may ask questions about sections they don't understand, before leaving the classroom.
3. Praise the children who have earned homework passes and tell them to take the passes home for the parents to see on the night that they do not want to do homework. Have them bring their passes to school the next day in lieu of homework and hand them in when homework is being collected.
4. When the first pass is used, make sure all students know about it and about the reason why it was used.

Rationale

1. The use of a homework pass encourages children to be more consistent in doing homework, as well as correctly.
2. It also tends to strengthen good work habits.

3. The turning in of assignments on time teaches the children responsibility.
4. Students are often punished for not doing their homework when it is not their fault, but the fault of their home environment. This technique gives the student an option or a positive way out of a dilemma.

FREE HOMEWORK PASS

Grades 5-6 / Maintaining Good Performance

Free Morning Or Afternoon

Situation
Some children in the class always complete their assignments correctly, neatly, and on time. You would like to reinforce this type of behavior on the part of all children in your class.

Strategy
1. Say to the class that the children whose names you will read have earned a free morning or afternoon for completing all their assignments neatly, correctly, and on time for the past two (or three) weeks.
2. These children may work anywhere in the building: the library, the principal's office, the gymnasium, rooms where interesting visual aids are being viewed or science experiments are being conducted, and in the Learning Center or at learning stations. The only requirement is that they keep a log of their activities and turn it in to you.
3. If children are to work in another room in the building, prior plans should be made with the person in charge of the room.
4. Collect the logs. Let the children share some of their interesting experiences with the rest of the class.

Rationale
1. The possibility of attaining a free morning can improve student work habits and performance.
2. Having a free morning can be a reinforcer for many children.
3. Permitting students to exercise options during a free morning can help them develop greater independence.
4. Having the school environment serve as a reinforcer provides the student with a positive concept of school.

Grades K-1 / Improving Class Attitudes

Good Start

Situation

You want children to have a favorable attitude about coming to school on the first day, and to have a minimum amount of fear.

Strategy

1. Have the mothers bring their children to school at the time of registration, prior to the first day of school.
2. While the mother is talking to the secretary and providing the needed registration information, have the principal come out of the office with a cookie jar and let the child choose a cookie from it. Also have the principal remark, "My, I'm glad to see you. I like you. I am glad that you will be coming to this school. Would you like to see some of the toys in my office?" Let the child see and hold stuffed animals, or toy cars, or airplanes that can be manipulated.
3. If there is time, the child might also be given a preview of his or her room and told how to find it.
4. Children may also be given several trial runs during the summer for finding the room.

Rationale

1. The use of cookies and praise by the principal can be quite reinforcing and reassuring to young children upon their first entry into the school environment.
2. The principal's individual attention helps the student feel wanted in the school and that it is a friendly environment.
3. The children can learn early that the principal's office need not be a threatening place.
4. The student will be slightly familiar and less threatened with the school environment by making visits before September.

Grades K-3 / Maintaining Good Performance

Good Workers

Situation
You want to improve the work habits of children as they are working independently at their seats, and while you are working with another group in the front of the room.

Strategy
1. Write the words "Good Workers" on the chalkboard.
2. In colored chalk write the names of the children who are working well at their seats. Write a new name about every five minutes.
3. If the child looks up, smile at that child while you are working with your group in the front of the room.

Rationale
1. This technique reinforces good work habits.
2. It permits all children an equal opportunity for gaining recognition.

Grades 3-6 / Disruptive Behavior

Guts

Situation

Jesse has no problem in class but has difficulty with unstructured situations such as recess, lunch, before, and after school. He usually punches or kicks other children. The teacher would like to eliminate Jesse's aggressive behavior.

Strategy

1. Set up a weekly chart for Jesse in which he gets one point for each time he doesn't fight in an unstructured situation. Be specific with him. Give him one point for nonaggressive behavior before school, one point for morning recess, one for lunch, one for afternoon recess, and one point for after school. This means that Jesse can earn as many as five points a day or twenty-five per week.
2. Praise Jesse when he behaves well during one of these intervals. Say, "I knew you had the guts to win," or if he goes for two periods without fighting, say, "That's two points in a row — nice going — you really have guts."
3. During the following week give Jesse a minute of privileges for every point he earns. (Example: twenty-one points equals twenty-one minutes with a counselor for fun and games, or let Jesse choose a friend and go to the back of the room to play a game of his choice.)
4. Encourage Jesse to try to beat his previous week's record of twenty-one points. Tell him that it is going to take a lot of guts to do it. If he wins tell him, "I knew you weren't a sissy, you really have guts."
5. Make Jesse your special helper the next day whenever he gets five out of five.
6. When Jesse carries something for you, let him know that he is strong.

Rationale
1. A point system can be used effectively for modifying a student's behavior.
2. Praise can also be used as additional reinforcer to change behavior.
3. Having a student compete against his own record is often more effective than competing with peers, because extensive peer competition can often heighten student anxiety and aggression.
4. Youngsters often associate fighting and manliness with "guts." It is important to reverse Jesse's thinking so that he associates "guts" with self-control.

Grades 2-4 / Inattentiveness

The Handshake

Situation

Alani is inattentive in mathematics classes. Consequently she does not give many right answers when called upon. You want her to be more attentive and improve her performance in class.

Strategy
1. Ask Alani a question in mathematics that you know she can answer.
2. When she gives the correct response, say to her, "That was a good answer. I am going to shake your hand."
3. Then shake her hand.
4. As she continues to give right answers, shake her hand again.
5. Use praise and a smile with the handshake as double reinforcers.
6. Shake other children's hands also in order that Alani is not singled out.

Rationale
1. Initially programming a child toward success can improve self-image and cause the child to make even greater academic strides.
2. A handshake is personal. It is one of the most effective reinforcers used by behaviorists.
3. A handshake coupled with praise and a smile provides an even more powerful reinforcer.

Grades 1-3 / Improving Mathematics Skills

The Happy Face

Situation
Your children do not know their number facts. You want them to improve in this respect.

Strategy
1. Give each child a piece of oaktag with a circular face drawn on it.
2. Tell the children that they will be given a star each time they learn five number facts. The stars can be used to form eyes, nose and mouth with teeth on a happy face. (The spaces for putting the stars should have been marked on the circle ahead of time.)
3. When the happy faces have been completed, the children can take them home to show their parents.

Rationale
1. Many children appear to enjoy being associated with a happy face.
2. The building of the happy face tends to be an ongoing positive reinforcer.
3. The opportunity to take the happy face home and to be praised tends to serve as a double positive reinforcer.

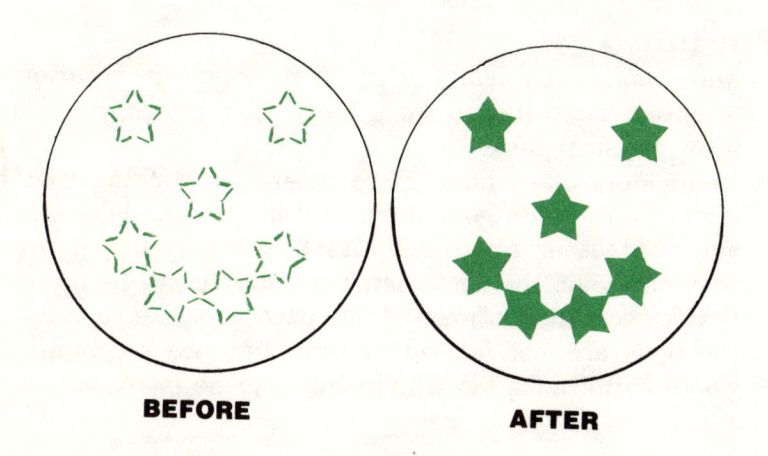

BEFORE   **AFTER**

Grades 5-6 / Attention Seeking

Help The Custodian

Situation
John and Robert are students who gain attention through showing off in class when your back is turned or when you are busy with other children. Their actions often influence other students to misbehave. Both boys enjoy helping the custodian.

Strategy
1. Tell John and Robert the kind of behavior you expect from them in the school environment. Be specific.
2. Break the school day into six hourly segments on a chart. (Or, some other segment of time.)
3. Give John and Robert one combined point for each hour that their behavior is acceptable.
4. Permit the boys to earn a possible total of six points a day with an extra bonus point for a perfect day.
5. Alert the custodian to the possibility of having helpers. Provide tips on how to be ego-supportive and ask that a few jobs be saved for the boys. Make certain that the tasks are commensurate with their strength and stamina, and that they are free of danger.
6. Let both boys help the custodian when they have accumulated a total of twenty-five combined points.

Rationale
1. Many nonacademically oriented students are vocationally oriented. They like to work with their hands and to perform physical tasks.
2. Youngsters often have more incentive working together toward a common goal. John and Robert can both encourage each other to accumulate the twenty-five points so they can visit the custodian together. It can be more fun that way. (Caution needs to be used to make certain that the boys are not fooling around, but are accomplishing worthwhile tasks for which they can be praised.)

Grades 4-6 / Disruptive Behavior

Homemade Ice Cream

Situation
You have a class that behaves poorly. No one in particular is the chief offender. The minor disturbances, however, are impeding the learning process of the total class.

Strategy
1. Obtain a secondhand machine for making ice cream.
2. Train a committee of three children to make the ice cream. (Use a homeroom mother to help if necessary.)
3. Treat the children to the ice cream when a special occasion warrants such a treat in order to interest children in ice cream as a reinforcer.
4. Let the children know that the next treat will be given for good behavior.
5. Make a contract with the children and let them know that when they earn one thousand points, a treat will be forthcoming.
6. Indicate further that each day will be broken into six one-hour segments. In each of the segments the class can earn a total of ten points for good behavior or a total of sixty points in a given day.
7. Let the children know that in each one-hour segment points will be awarded as follows:
    a. Ten points will be given if the class behaves and no one has to be reminded about breaking a rule.
    b. Nine points will be given if only one person has to be reminded about an infraction of a rule. Eight will be given for two people, etc.
8. Post the number of points the class has earned each day on a chart or calendar.
9. Praise the children for the number of points they have earned each hour and at the end of each day.
10. Treat the class when the one thousand points have been earned.

11. Say, "I am proud of this class. It took a lot of hard work and effort to earn one thousand points. You are terrific. I am proud to be your teacher."

Rationale
1. Food, and ice cream in particular, can be an effective positive reinforcer to bring about a change in the behavior of children.
2. An hourly and daily account helps to build up student enthusiasm toward obtaining the goal.
3. Continual praise also helps to motivate children toward good behavior.
4. The approach used in this situation locks children into patterns leading to success. If they do not earn enough points in four weeks, they can continue to earn the points needed for reaching their goal.
5. Achieving a high number of points, such as one thousand, usually has a positive effect on children. It gives them a sense of accomplishment.
6. Having children make homemade ice cream as a class has a variety of implications for additional kinds of teaching.

Grades 4-6 / Disruptive Behavior

Individual Activities

Situation
Dena is hyperactive in the classroom. She distracts other children and annoys the teacher. Her classmates and the teacher have negative feelings toward her. The psychologist diagnosed Dena as a bright, hyperemotional student who could use her nervous energies to produce a considerable amount of schoolwork in a short period of time.

Strategy
1. Prescribe an individualized program of instruction for
2. Place a study carrel in an isolated area of the classroom where Dena can do her work for two hours daily.
3. Make certain that Dena understands that this is not a form of rejection, but it is a way for her to be highly productive.
4. Praise Dena when she completes her assignments.
5. Send a note to Dena's parents on the first day that she does well in her work.
6. Integrate Dena gradually into the regular classroom group for longer periods of time when she starts demonstrating the ability to work independently without annoying others.

Rationale
1. If a student has intelligence and drive, his or her energy usually can be constructively channeled into productivity.
2. Moving Dena into a carrel is a form of environmental manipulation and can have several benefits. It prevents her from disturbing other children and having them angry with her, and it cuts down on the external stimuli affecting Dena, enabling her to concentrate on her work.
3. Praise serves to further positively reinforce Dena.

Grades 3-5 / Inadequate Academic Performance

Individual Motivation Chart

Situation
Patrick, a nine year old, does very little seatwork. As an outgrowth of his past school experiences, he has developed a failure syndrome. Pat hates school and almost everything associated with it. Pat likes race cars.

Strategy
1. Draw a racetrack on a sheet of oaktag.
2. Divide the track into four segments.
3. Permit Pat to bring his favorite small toy car to class.
4. Explain to Pat that each time he completes a seatwork assignment he can move his car one segment on the racetrack.
5. Tell Pat that when he reaches the finish line on the track, he will be given an opportunity to choose an activity for himself from a variety of options.
6. When Pat completes his assignments reinforce him according to the contract made with him.

Rationale
1. Several positive reinforcers can operate in this situation:
    a. Pat can be given an opportunity to bring something he likes to school and use it in a game-like situation.
    b. Participating in the game or having Pat move his car forward can cause him to work even harder on his succeeding assignments in order to reach the finish line.
    c. Reaching the finish line can give Pat a sense of accomplishment.
    d. Choosing his own final activity from a series of options makes that activity important for Pat.

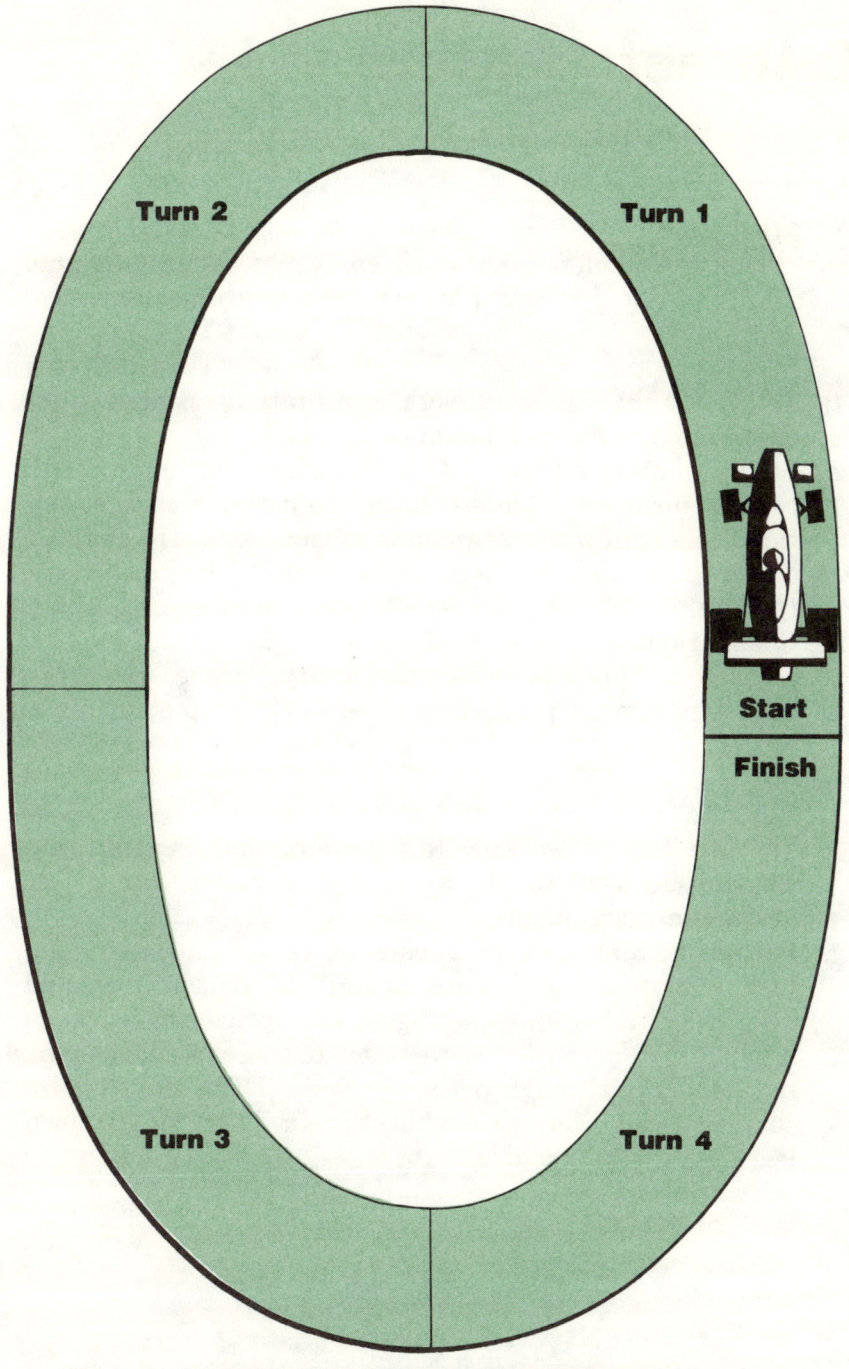

Track can be arranged in smaller segments according to the needs of the child. Reinforcement should occur frequently.

Grades 2-6 / Leisure Time

Interest Centers

Situation
Betty usually completes her work early. She often gets into trouble if additional meaningful experiences are not provided.

Strategy
1. Tell Betty that she may work in an interest center of her choice as a reinforcer for finishing early.
2. Set up in different parts of the room interest centers with colorful displays of games, stories to be completed, activities, crossword puzzles, and audiovisual aids. The interest centers may cover subject areas of math, language arts, reading, social studies, science, and the arts.
3. Completion of projects at the interest center can only be counted as bonus points toward Betty's grade.
4. Give Betty extra grade credit for work completed in the center.

Rationale
1. The privilege of working in an interesting learning center can be used to get a child to complete other less attractive assignments.
2. Letting a child work in a learning center on meaningful tasks can heighten enthusiasm about school work and keep the child from engaging in disruptive activities.
3. A choice of activities serves the purpose of developing independence through decision making. The child is also sharing the power with a teacher in directing her own learning.

Grades 5-6 / Improving Class Attitudes

The Interesting Question

Situation
You want to heighten students' interest and improve their work habits.

Strategy
1. Write on the chalkboard in colored chalk a question, such as, "In all the world, where can you find strawberries that grow the size of peaches?"
2. When the students start noticing the question and start asking for the answer, tell them that you will give them the answer at the end of the morning or afternoon when all the assigned work has been completed.
3. Go up to the chalkboard periodically throughout the morning or afternoon, look at the question and look back at the children.
4. When the students say, "Come on, tell us the answer now," indicate to them that they will be given the answer as soon as the class assignments are completed correctly.

Rationale
1. The answer to an interesting question can be used effectively to sustain student interest and performance.
2. In this case students will work harder to complete tasks in order to have time at the end of the day to discuss the question that has aroused their curiosity.

Grades 1-3 / Improving Reading Skills

Intermittent Reinforcement

Situation
When you are working with a reading group, you notice that James dawdles and does not get his assignments completed at his seat.

Strategy
1. Give your reading group a page to read silently.
2. Move back to James' seat quickly.
3. Praise him for the work that he has completed.
4. Encourage him to continue working by saying something like, "I bet that you will have a lot more done by the time that I look at your papers again."
5. Repeat the procedure at periodic intervals each day.

Rationale
1. Intermittent reinforcement is used in this situation to encourage James to work consistently and to complete his assignments.
2. The teacher's praise and extra attention tends to motivate James and improve his self-image, as well as to enhance his position with his peers.

Grades 5-6 / Improving Class Attitudes

Keep Away

Situation
You feel that Ernestine doesn't like you. She may even have reason to have negative feelings toward you, because you put many Xs on her papers. You can hardly praise her because she's a very poor student who has few right answers. You are concerned about her academic performance and attitude toward you.

Strategy
1. Choose Ernestine, one other class member, and recruit someone from the school staff to play "Keep Away" with you against the rest of your class on an area the size of a football field.
2. The game simply is for your team to pass a ball back and forth on the run, keeping it away from the class. If the class has the ball you must chase them.
3. As you're playing, shout encouraging remarks to Ernestine: "Nice pass," "Way to go," "Good hustle."

Rationale
1. Being chosen for the teacher's team is often interpreted by students as "My teacher likes me."
2. Your praise during the game is usually ego-supportive and honest. Most often children will play and try hard if they are on the teacher's team. Children basically want to be liked by their teacher. Letting Ernestine be on your team in game situations should help your relationship with her.

Grades 1-3 / Inadequate Academic Performance

King And Queen For The Day

Situation
You want to improve classroom performance.

Strategy
1. Put your class on a point system based upon performance.
2. As soon as the first boy and girl have earned twenty points, permit them to wear crowns that you have previously made.
3. Call them "King and Queen" for the day.
4. If there is a tie, have more than one boy and girl wear crowns, making "Kings and Queens" for the day.

Rationale
1. Wearing a crown positively reinforces many children.
2. This technique also gives good achievers who are often overlooked a chance to feel important.

55

Grades 2-5 / Disruptive Behavior

Kitchen Timer

Situation
Your class is out of control. You want the children to start behaving appropriately.

Strategy
1. Tell the children that they may earn items from a table for proper behavior and for assignments that are completed properly.
2. Let the children know that items may be earned by acquiring tokens that have buying power.
3. Allocate the number of tokens children must earn for each item.
4. Set a kitchen timer with a bell that goes off at irregular intervals. When the bell goes off, give each child a token if he is performing as expected.
5. Let the children cash in the tokens for the items at the end of the morning.
6. While the other children are enjoying the options they have earned with their free time, work with the members of the class who have not earned sufficient tokens.

Rationale
1. A kitchen timer can be an effective device for helping students develop self-management skills.
2. Having the timer go off at irregular intervals causes children to be more conscious of their actions and attempt to engage in more acceptable behavior.
3. Tokens are effective with students when they have buying power.

Grades 4-6 / Disruptive Behavior

Kits

Situation
Alfred has not learned sufficient self-management skills. Consequently he has difficulty controlling himself during non-structured times, such as recess. He does not abide by school rules or the rules of most games. He also engages in many arguments and fights. Alfred likes to work with kits, such as painting-by-numbers, mosaics, and models of automobiles, etc.

Strategy
1. Discuss with Alfred your concerns about his behavior.
2. Let him know the specific kinds of behavior you prefer.
3. Tell Alfred that you will permit him to earn five points for good behavior during each unstructured time block throughout the school day. When he earns twenty-five points, he may work with a kit.
4. Permit Alfred to choose a friend to work with him.
5. Praise Alfred often for good behavior and for his models.

Rationale
1. A child's behavior can often be changed when the change leads to engaging in an activity which he likes.
2. Working with kits is often a positive reinforcer and can be used to produce behavioral changes.
3. Points can be used as immediate reinforcers until the major reinforcer is received.
4. Praise usually helps children build their self-image.
5. Many commercial hobbies and crafts are easily made into attractive finished products, which give youngsters much satisfaction and a sense of pride. Professional looking results can appreciably raise a child's self-image.
6. Children often resist art projects, feeling incapable of producing anything worthwhile. Working with commercial hobby kits makes many children more enthusiastic about art projects and about their own capabilities.

Grades K-3 / Self-Image

The Lift

Situation

Barry is a boy who lacks confidence. You want to build up his classroom performance.

Strategy
1. Observe Barry's oral and written work.
2. Take note of when Barry has shown some improvement and say, "I am very pleased with the amount of improvement you made. Stand up."
3. Take Barry's two arms and lift him up. If he does not get frightened, lift him above your head and say, "You make me feel ten feet tall. How does it feel to be ten feet tall?"
4. Remember that if the experience is enjoyable and gives Barry some status, he may request to be lifted many times. The lifting should then become contingent upon improved classroom performance.

Rationale
1. Many children enjoy being lifted into the air.
2. Children also enjoy the close proximity and touching by an adult, as well as words of praise and encouragement. Such attention may prove to be a powerful positive reinforcer.

Grades K-5 / Disruptive Behavior

Love Notes

Situation
Betty Ann's behavior in the classroom is erratic. You want to improve her behavior and involve her parents in the process.

Strategy
1. When Betty Ann's behavior has been acceptable send home a "love note" telling her parents about the improved behavior.
2. Suggest that the parents praise her or give her an extra privilege such as watching television for fifteen extra minutes that night.

Rationale
1. "Love notes" can be effective instruments for producing behavioral changes. They utilize praise most effectively.
2. In too many instances parents are notified only when a child misbehaves. As a result parents often feel threatened by school authorities and do not look upon the school with favor. Such feelings hamper parent-school relationships and can have negative effects upon the child. Those effects can often heighten rather than lessen the problems the school has with the child.

Grades 1-5 / Inadequate Academic Performance

Lunch With The Principal

Situation
You want Sabrena to improve her test performances in spelling, math, reading, etc.

Strategy
1. When Sabrena shows the slightest improvement over previous test scores, praise her.
2. Have all teachers at grade level praise her.
3. Have the principal praise her.
4. Tell Sabrena that she may invite the principal to have lunch at her table in the cafeteria after more significant improvement is shown.
5. While having lunch with Sabrena and the other children, have the principal mention with pride the improvement Sabrena has made in her test scores.
6. Remember, the chances are that if the children enjoy having the principal at their table, they will encourage Sabrena to continue her pattern of improvement.

Rationale
1. Lunch with the principal can be an excellent positive reinforcer with many children.
2. Sabrena feels secure with the principal sitting next to her.
3. Sitting next to the student usually suggests that the principal likes him or her.
4. Sabrena's classmates will usually express appreciation to Sabrena because it was she who caused the principal to have lunch with the group.
5. This is a particularly good idea for the student who may be having peer group problems.

Grade 1-3 / Self-Image

The Magic Touch

Situation
Lori is a child who gets upset before tests and consequently does not do well on them. You want her to relax and improve her test performance.

Strategy
1. Say to Lori, "I am going to give you the magic touch, and I know that you will do much better on this test."
2. Touch Lori on the forehead with your index finger.
3. Positively reinforce Lori further by smiling at her during the test or even winking at her.
4. Say, "See, I knew you could do better," at the end of the test.

Rationale
1. The "Magic Touch" is a silent signal of approval to a child. It indicates that you have confidence in her.
2. The power of positive thinking is being transferred to Lori in this approach. The "Magic Touch" plants the suggestion that she can improve.
3. Touch, facial expressions and verbal reinforcement are used in concert to support Lori.

Grades K-3 / Inattentiveness

The Mail Carrier

Situation
You want to improve classroom attentiveness and performance.

Strategy
1. Tell the children that the first person whose work is done correctly may take the attendance register to the principal's office.
2. Make a mail carrier's hat and pouch for that child. Praise the child for completing the work neatly and correctly.
3. Permit the next three children to go along as mail guards in order to reinforce them. Have the secretary praise all of them when they come to the office.
4. Have the mail carrier choose his or her own guards or another child to accompany him as a variation. When they arrive at the principal's office, they should be rewarded with praise or a cookie.

Rationale
1. By using the "Mail Carrier" you are motivating the child to work swiftly but carefully.
2. This is an opportunity to positively reinforce the accelerated student's performance.
3. It is also an opportunity for the child to receive praise from those who work in the school offices.

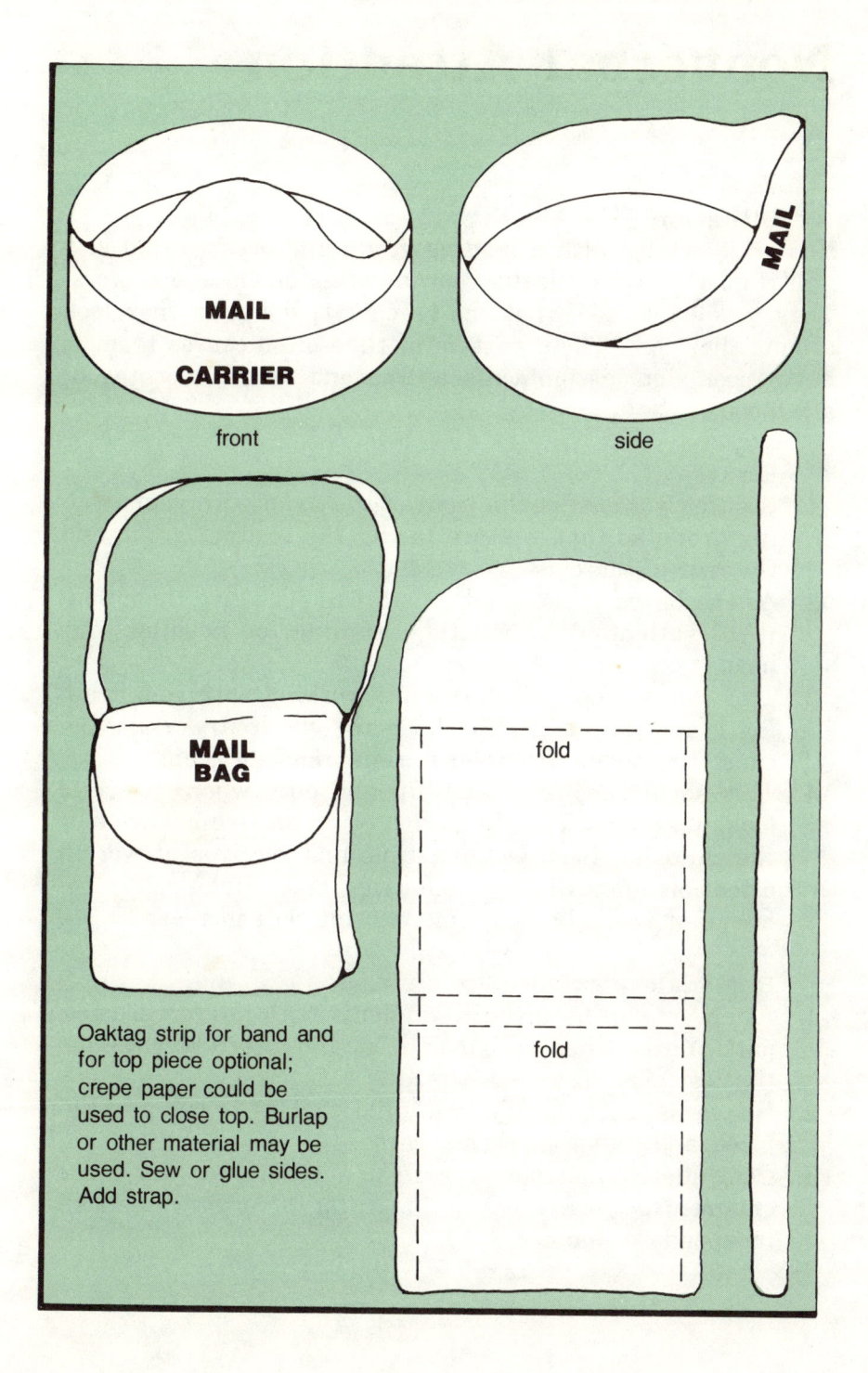

MAIL CARRIER

front

side

MAIL BAG

fold

fold

Oaktag strip for band and for top piece optional; crepe paper could be used to close top. Burlap or other material may be used. Sew or glue sides. Add strap.

Grades 1-3 / Inattentiveness

Nonverbal Attention

Situation

You are working with a reading group and observe that several children have difficulty concentrating on their seat work. They look up to see what the teacher is doing or they look around the room. Their wasting of time often causes them to have incomplete assignments at the end of the morning or afternoon.

Strategy

1. Position yourself at the front of the room with your reading group so that you are facing the reading group and the rest of the class.
2. As the heads of the children start to rise, give them nonverbal attention by winking, smiling, or nodding your head.
3. This can be done while you are working with your reading group. It can usually keep the children working because the added attention is reinforcing to them.
4. This should be used carefully and only when the child looks up after a lengthy period of productive behavior. If the child has been wasting time and receives nonverbal attention immediately following this undesirable behavior it is likely that time-wasting will increase.

Rationale

1. Attention can be given to students with nonverbal cues, particularly when verbal ones might interrupt class activities.
2. Nonverbal cues signify to a child that he is being recognized and that the teacher cares.
3. Continual reinforcement with nonverbal cues can cause children to work an entire morning or afternoon in an independent manner.

Grades 2-6 / Inadequate Academic Performance

The Number Right

Situation
On her weekly spelling tests Sadie gets sixteen, seventeen, or eighteen words wrong out of a total of twenty. You want Sadie to get more words right each week.

Strategy
1. Concentrate on the number Sadie gets right each week and make her feel good about those by praising her.
2. Say to her, "I am very pleased that you got four words right this week. I know that you will work hard next week and will probably get five or six words right."
3. Help Sadie to make a visual chart or graph on which she can mark the number she receives right each week.
4. If the student usually has more than half of the words wrong, then the amount presented each week should probably be reduced to a figure that is within the range of the child's capacity.

Rationale
1. The chart emphasizes the number of Sadie's correct responses rather than emphasizing the number wrong.
2. This technique places the emphasis upon the number right and usually causes the child to improve the score from week to week.
3. Verbal praise is encouraging to Sadie and helps her to realize that the teacher is supportive of her actions.
4. Children are often eager to engage in work that is represented on self-goal charts as in this example.

Grades K-3 / Self-Image

The Nurse

Situation
It is the first day of school and Harold, a new student, is crying hysterically. He does not want to come into his classroom.

Strategy
1. Let Harold's mother know this behavior is not unusual. Attempt to put her at ease.
2. Tell Harold and his mother that if Harold stops crying, he will be allowed to help the nurse.
3. Ask the mother to walk Harold to the nurse's office.
4. Inform the nurse beforehand that you may be sending her a hysterical child. She should be ready with a few easy tasks for the child.
5. Have the child complete the tasks with the nurse while the mother is present. After he is absorbed in the task, tell Harold that his mother will have to leave and will see him at lunch time. Ask the mother to leave.
6. Have the nurse eventually walk Harold to his classroom.
7. Attempt to work him into the normal routine of the class. If this does not work immediately, it may be necessary for Harold to spend more than a day with the nurse.
8. Remember in extreme cases of hysteria, the child may also need supportive psychiatric services. In these cases of hysteria it may be advantageous for the mother to remain within Harold's view for a longer period of time.

Rationale
1. The first school contact should be a happy one. This can be achieved better through individual attention that cannot be given by the teacher.
2. A nurse can be used in many ways on the first day of school to influence better adjustment for some children.

Grades 4-6 / Inattentiveness

Old Curiosity Cupboard

Situation
You want to improve children's attention span and classroom performance.

Strategy
1. Set aside a cupboard in your room and call it the "Old Curiosity Cupboard."
2. Put on the shelves in the cupboard a variety of items that would be of interest to your children. The items should be the kind that they can touch and manipulate. They could be *National Geographic* magazines, samples of ore, samples of products from other countries, or materials for science experiments.
3. When a child has performed well, say, "You may have five minutes with materials from the Curiosity Cupboard."
4. Vary the times during which a child may have materials from the Old Curiosity Cupboard. For example, if you decide to excuse a child or several children from a quiz, you might want to give them thirty or forty minutes to work with materials from the cupboard.

Rationale
1. The element of surprise is the effective positive reinforcer in this technique. Children are curious by nature and will work to have an opportunity to use the materials in the Curiosity Cupboard.
2. The hands-on approach is fun for children; therefore they will try to extend their attention span and improve classroom performance so they may visit it.
3. The Old Curiosity Cupboard can be used to give children instant reinforcement at a time when they are not expecting it, and can cause others to be even more attentive throughout a particular lesson.

Grades 1-4 / Tardiness And Absenteeism

On Time

Situation
Luisa is continually late for school. You want to reinforce her coming to school on time.

Strategy
1. Praise Luisa when she does come to school on time and let her know that you are proud of her.
2. Have the children clap for Luisa so that she knows they are proud of her when she is in school on time.
3. Stop the clapping when Luisa develops the habit of coming to school on time.

Rationale
1. Praise can be used to positively reinforce promptness.
2. Clapping can also reinforce promptness. It serves as a double positive reinforcer.

Grades 2-4 / Social Skills

Our Friend

Situation
The students are name-calling and degrading each other. You want them to be friendlier, more tolerant, and more understanding.

Strategy
1. Write the word "Friend" on the chalkboard in colored chalk.
2. Have the children state characteristics that make another child a friend.
3. Write those characteristics on the chalkboard, again with colored chalk.
4. Have the children select a classmate who has likeable characteristics to go to the front of the room.
5. Give the children an opportunity to tell why they like the chosen classmate, using the characteristics on the chalkboard as a guide.
6. Have all the students clap for the chosen person.
7. Continue the process of selecting a different student each day until all the students in the class have received recognition.
8. Have the student wear an "Our Friend" banner.
9. Take the student's picture. Paste it at the top of a chart alongside his name and above a list of his likeable characteristics. Do this as a possible variation in the technique.

Rationale
1. Wearing a banner or having a picture on display can be a positive reinforcer.
2. It is important to condition students to think positively about each other. In too many instances students with poor self-concepts tend to degrade their peers in an attempt to place themselves on a higher level.

3. The process gives recognition to the students for their likeable characteristics and tends to reinforce those characteristics.
4. It gives all students an equal opportunity for being made to feel important at some time during the school year.

Cut out 2 pieces of material.   Sew together.   Add lettering.

Grades 3-5 / Disruptive Behavior

Partners

Situation
A majority of the teachers in your school have indicated their dissatisfaction with general classroom behavior. They feel that with better control, more learning can take place.

Strategy
1. Request the aid of a neighboring teacher to work with you as a team on improving classroom behavior.
2. Discuss your concerns with your class and make a contract with them based on the following:
   a. At irregular intervals teacher A, your neighbor, will enter the classroom.
   b. If no students are misbehaving, the class will receive ten points.
   c. If one student is misbehaving, the class receives nine.
   d. The observing neighboring teacher indicates to you the number of points earned. Write the number on a chart that is visible to the class.
   e. Reverse the procedure. Go into the neighboring teacher's room the same number of times.
3. Use accumulated points for short and long range rewards. Initially, the class should determine what the short and long range positive reinforcers should be in accordance with the number of points earned.

Rationale
1. The system is arranged so the class can win. If two youngsters are misbehaving, then the majority of the class is still behaving and deserves eight points.
2. Team efforts are more effective than individual efforts.
3. If the children select their own positive reinforcer, they will work harder for it.
4. Often an entire class is punished because the minority misbehaves. The "Partners" plan reverses this trend.

Grades 3-6 / Attention Seeking

Peer Tutor

Situation

Taras is a boy who cannot work independently for long periods of time. After working for a while he becomes restless and then begins to engage in disruptive forms of behavior that disturb other children in the classroom.

Strategy
1. Ask Taras if he would like to become a tutor or teacher assistant.
2. Tell him that the job is contingent upon completion of his reading seat work.
3. Let him read with his own group first, work on his seatwork next, and then tutor another student or help the teacher with a slower group.

Rationale
1. Serving as a tutor or teacher assistant can be a positive reinforcer for many children.
2. It channels a child's energies into more productive activities.
3. It gives a child an opportunity to be praised for worthwhile behavior and the performance of a service needed in the classroom.
4. It creates better pupil-teacher relationships.
5. It gives a child attention and status for positive forms of behavior.

Grades 3-6 / Improving Mathematics Skills

Peer Tutoring

Situation
Autherine does her work but she is very careless in completing it, particularly her math.

Strategy
1. Tell Autherine that you realize she is a good student and that Mrs. Burke may need help with her younger students.
2. Have Autherine sign a contract which states that upon the accurate completion of her math, she may go to Mrs. Burke's room on that day to help the younger children.
3. The teacher and Mrs. Burke must sign the contract to give it significance.
4. Permit Autherine to tutor when she fulfills her contract.

Rationale
1. It is reinforcing for a student to feel that he or she has helped another student.
2. A student enjoys helping another and often learns better from a peer than from an adult. There is less pressure, and the teaching and learning is based on the child's perspective, not the adult's.
3. A tutor often learns as much as the child who is being tutored.

Grades 4-6 / Disruptive Behavior

Physical Education Reward

Situation
Emanuel is an aggressive student who is constantly in fights. He also doesn't pay attention in the reading group.

Strategy
1. Ask Emanuel what he would like to do most during physical education class.
2. Sign a contract with Emanuel stating that for each effective reading lesson he performs you will let him be the quarterback for the team, or whatever he stipulates in his contract.
3. Make certain that Emanuel signs the contract.

Rationale
1. Often boys are not permitted to have a physical reward for a positive reinforcer. Yet it may be what they desire. Teachers must be especially aware of these needs in aggressive boys and girls.
2. Since boys are usually punished more often than girls for physical aggression, this aggression may indicate their need for physical activities.

Grades 1-3 / Disruptive Behavior

Picture A Day

Situation
Asunción is difficult to control in class. She is continually talking and making disruptive noises to gain attention.

Strategy
1. Speak to Asunción and find out what she likes to do when she has free time.
2. Make a contract with her that states that as soon as she finishes her work each day, she can make a drawing for the principal, if she likes to draw.
3. Have the secretary in the office praise her for her picture.
4. Have the principal praise Asunción for her picture and hang it near the office for public display.

Rationale
1. The contract is the motivating factor that can modify Asunción's behavior.
2. Asunción cannot talk and disrupt the class and still get her work completed on time.
3. The added attention Asunción receives in the office can reinforce her for it serves to raise her self-concept.

Grades 4-6 / Disruptive Behavior

Pitcher-Catcher

Situation
Arnold is a foster child trapped in an environment that does little to meet his social and emotional needs. Arnold would like to play Little League baseball but his parents won't allow him to play. They are very strict, controlling, and particularly punitive. Arnold's school is the outlet for his frustrations and he acts out aggressively on numerous occasions.

Strategy
1. Give Arnold a point for each day he doesn't fight.
2. Make each point worth 5 minutes with the teacher, counselor, or some other interested adult.
3. When Arnold accumulates enough points, take him to the gymnasium or other open area in the building where there is approximately 30 feet of space.
4. Rolls up 3 pairs of socks into a ball, put down a homeplate and let Arnold pitch the ball to you. Play the parts of the catcher and the umpire. Give Arnold a good target with your hands and when he pitches the ball (socks) say loudly "Strike" or "Ball." Be more emphatic on *Strike*.
5. Repeat this process weekly.

Rationale
1. Arnold will now have a reason not to fight, as he has the opportunity to do something he enjoys as a reward for controlling himself.
2. Throwing the ball hard will release much of Arnold's tension. This approach is a good outlet for Arnold's aggressive feelings.
3. Arnold could also be counseled while you are playing ball with him. Children are less inhibited in a play situation and often more verbal.

Grades 4-6 / Disruptive Behavior

Pizza

Situation

The teacher is dissatisfied with Hathleen's behavior. She talks in class, does very little work, and constantly disrupts other children who are working. Pizza is one of her favorite foods.

Strategy
1. Schedule a conference with Hathleen's parents and tell them of your concern.
2. Enlist their support. Ask them if they would buy Hathleen a pizza if she does well in school.
3. Break the day into segments of one hour.
4. Give Hathleen a ticket for each hour she behaves and put your signature and the date on it.
5. When Hathleen accumulates twenty-five tickets, have her take the tickets home. Start the system on a Monday so she can win on either Thursday or Friday. Her parents should take her out for a pizza in reward for the twenty-five tickets she brings home.
6. Remember, eventually Hathleen may want to change to some other food. Possibly her parents could take Hathleen out for spaghetti, hamburger, etc. for the accumulation of twenty-five tickets, as a variation in the reinforcer.

Rationale
1. Most children like pizza. For some children food is the most attractive positive reinforcer, and they will work hardest to obtain it.
2. This system is a way of involving Hathleen's parents with her positive behavior. They now hear from the school when Hathleen is doing well. In the usual situation, parents hear from the school only when their youngster has done something wrong.

Grade 1-2 / Improving Reading Skills

Play Money

Situation
Your children have short attention spans. You want to build up the attention span and performance level, particularly with letter and word recognition in reading.

Strategy
1. Tape a business size envelope to the front side of each child's desk. Do not put it on top of the desk, because the child might play with it.
2. Make small paper dollars about 2" × 5" in size.
3. When a child gives a correct response put a paper dollar in his or her envelope.
4. At the end of the morning, let the children count their dollars.
5. The dollars can be used for purchasing privileges or items from a table of positive reinforcers which may be used during recess time.
6. During the Easter season, you might want to make "Bunny Money," by drawing or pasting a rabbit on each dollar bill.

Rationale
1. Giving the children play money communicates to them in a nonverbal way that they have performed correctly and that the teacher is pleased with their performance.
2. It is another way of telling children that paying attention is important in the classroom.
3. Nonverbal reinforcement can be used effectively when a teacher wants to reinforce a child without interrupting the class or the flow of a lesson.

Grades 4-6 / Disruptive Behavior

The Point Game

Situation

The science class comes into your room noisily. Children continually talk when a question is asked. You want your class to come into the room quietly, settle down, start working, and continue working throughout the period without talking.

Strategy
1. Tell the children that you are going to play a game with them. The game will involve rows of children. When all children in a row come into the room quietly, they will earn a point for their row.
2. Mention that points can also be earned throughout the science period each day for correct responses and proper behavior.
3. Count the number of points that each row has earned at the end of each period. (At all times the points should be recorded on the chalkboard so that children can see the number of points their row is earning throughout each period.)
4. Make certain that at the end of the week, the row with the greatest number of points is excused from the weekly quiz and given the grade of "A" for the quiz. In addition, each person in the row is given options of working in one of five interesting learning stations that have been set up in the back of the room. This work would be done while others are taking the weekly quiz. It serves as a double reinforcer for children.
5. Change the composition of the rows each week by having students move over one seat with the student on the end moving to a vacant seat in another row.

Rationale
1. This is an effective use of the reinforcement of rows of children to improve the overall behavior of the class.

2. Children in each row tend to help encourage others in their row to engage in acceptable behavioral patterns to earn the weekly reinforcers.
3. Receiving a grade of "A" for a quiz and being permitted to work in learning stations can be reinforcers of satisfaction to students.
4. The use of points causes the students to see progress that their row is making and serves as a daily reinforcer, particularly if there is not a broad expanse of points among the rows. Keeping the rows close to each other in points from Monday to Friday heightens the enthusiasm to win.
5. Even if a particular row does not win, individual students in those rows can still earn an "A" grade on the weekly quiz.
6. The calmer learning atmosphere and the added attention throughout the week should permit the children to learn more. Also, more children might earn grades of "A."

Grades 4-6 / Inadequate Academic Performance

Principal's Helper

Situation
Kathy's parents recently separated. She blames her mother for Dad's leaving. She tries to get back at her mother by acting up in school. Her mother's first priority is for Kathy to do well in school, so Kathy attempts to punish her by not doing well and embarrassing her mother.

Strategy
1. Set up an individual contract with Kathy, permitting her to earn points for good behavior.
2. Give her one point for good behavior in the morning, and another for good behavior in the afternoon.
3. Let Kathy be the principal's special helper when she earns ten points. (The principal should save a few jobs for Kathy.)
4. Have the principal praise Kathy when she finishes helping by saying, "It's good to have dependable helpers around. I have been so busy lately, I certainly appreciate you helping me with my work." A handshake or pat on the head on the way out of the office is recommended.

Rationale
1. Little can be done by a teacher concerning relationships in a student's home. The teacher should concentrate on helping the student achieve satisfaction in school.
2. Children must feel useful and worthy. It usually gives them great pleasure to have the distinction of being the principal's helper. There is only one principal in the school building, and attention is being received from that special person.
3. Praise, a pat, or a handshake from the principal can also be positively reinforcing.
4. Kathy can reap reinforcement for positive behavior. She can also feel better toward authority figures.

Grades 1-3 / Incomplete Classwork

The Principal's Office

Situation
Paul is a boy who wastes a considerable amount of time and does not complete his classroom assignments each morning. He has often been kept in during recess and made to complete assignments, but that has not been too successful. You are looking for an alternative plan.

Strategy
1. Make a contract with Paul whereby he can earn extra points during four time blocks in the morning.
2. If he earns four points, he may go to the principal's office and bring back an item that the class can borrow for a day. Examples of items might be a starfish, a stuffed animal, a ball, a book, or a game.
3. If Paul has earned only three points for a given day, he may choose an alternate positive reinforcer.
4. When Paul visits the office, make certain that the secretary and the principal praise him.
5. For an added positive reinforcer, let Paul take a friend with him and play on the office carpet for five minutes with a toy or game they choose.

Rationale
1. Verbal praise will lessen Paul's hostility.
2. The earning of points can be positively reinforcing, especially when total points can purchase privileges.
3. The principal can be of valuable assistance when using positive approaches in dealing with children.
4. Permitting Paul to bring a friend to the office enhances his social relationships.
5. Earning items which can be used in the classroom further enhances Paul's social relationships.
6. The class can help by continually encouraging Paul. Some classmates may even wish to tutor him.

Grades K-3 / Attention Seeking

Proximity

Situation
Raymond is a boy who continually seeks attention by engaging in disruptive acts. He often arouses other students and stimulates them into misbehavior. You want to change Raymond's behavior.

Strategy
1. Observe Raymond's behavior.
2. Before Raymond starts to get restless, move over toward Raymond's seat and teach the class from there.
3. Put your hand on his shoulder or on top of his head and continue teaching.
4. Move back to the front of the room as Raymond becomes more settled. Initially it may be necessary to move near Raymond several times a day. This should be done consistently before Raymond gets restless.
5. The teacher should be careful not to move over immediately following undesirable behavior, as doing so might increase the frequency of this behavior.

Rationale
1. The proximity of a teacher to a child affects a child's feelings about the child's relationship to the teacher.
2. Having a teacher move near to a child can cause the child to feel important and believe that the teacher likes the child. It may also cause a child to be more attentive to the lesson by heightening feelings of self-worth.
3. Touching can also be positively reinforcing, particularly if accompanied by a smile.
4. There is likely to be an increase in Raymond's working behavior and a decrease in his disruptive behavior.

Grades 2-6 / Maintaining Good Performance

The Punching Bag

Situation
You want to reinforce children's good work habits and correct responses.

Strategy
1. Obtain a punching bag on a stand and install it in a corner of your classroom.
2. Tell the children that they will have opportunities for punching the bag when they have given an outstanding response to a question or for the improvement of skills.
3. Throughout the day, reinforce the children by praising them and giving them opportunities for punching the bag.

Rationale
1. This is a fine way to reinforce skills and behavior through pleasurable activity.
2. This technique channels excessive energy into positive directions. Boys particularly enjoy it.
3. It can also be used to reduce tension and aggressiveness.
4. It is far better for a child to punch a bag than to punch a classmate.

Grades 3-6 / Disruptive Behavior

Quiet Corners

Situation
A group of students in your classroom is continually noisy and disruptive. You would like to eliminate the disruptions by having the students modify their own behavior.

Strategy
1. Call the disruptive students together and frankly discuss your concerns about their behavior.
2. Tell them that you are confident that they are grown up enough to change their behavior.
3. Indicate that if they feel the need for bothering their neighbors, they may move themselves into the "Quiet Corners" where they will not disturb anyone or be disturbed while working on their assignments.
4. Set up as many attractive "Quiet Corners" as needed. Use physical dividers to set them apart.

Rationale
1. The "Quiet Corners" approach helps students to become more responsible for changing their own behaviors.
2. Self-modifying techniques are often a better means of changing behavior than those that are forced upon children by teachers. They are also of greater longevity.

Grades 3-6 / Improving Reading Skills

Racetrack

Situation
Few of the students in your class are reading independently. You would like to motivate them to do more reading on their own.

Strategy
1. Place two large oaktag sheets with racetracks drawn on them in front of the room. Have the boys and girls select what they would like to race: horses or automobiles.
2. Have the students trace a pattern and cut out their own horses or automobiles.
3. Allow each student to color the car or horse if desired, and to put a favorite number on it.
4. Divide the tracks into forty sections. Each time a student reads a book, have the student move the car or horse forward a section. For books over 100 pages have the car or horse moved two sections.
5. Race the horses or cars on separate tracks.
6. Give a student a small reward when halfway around the track, and a larger one when the student crosses the finish line.
7. Racing with other students may be too competitive and the poor student with a lowered self-image may again view herself or himself as a loser. Therefore, it may be more desirable to have separate tracks for some students.

Rationale
1. Progress is more meaningful to many students if they are able to visualize it.
2. Children enjoy the independence of managing their own activities. It is usually more effective than controlled reinforcement.
3. Many children are by nature competitive and will read books so they can beat others around the track.

87

START
FINISH

HALF-
WAY

Grades 1-2 / Improving Reading Skills

Reading Train

Situation
You want your children to do more reading and to improve their performance of reading skills.

Strategy
1. Make an engine and a caboose out of cardboard boxes.
2. Set them up along a wall of the classroom with space between them.
3. Place regular reading chairs between the engine and the caboose to resemble seats on a train. Face them forward or toward the engine.
4. Tell the children that they may ride on the "reading train" and read books there, provided that their reading seatwork has been completed accurately.
5. Have student conductors or an "engineer" check the reading seatwork before a child may ride the train. The conductors or engineer should be students in the class who normally do well in reading.
6. plane after you have had a reading train for a month or checked a child's paper, the teacher should also check the paper later on. Checking errors can be lessened by using answer sheets or "test keys."
7. Using different boxes, rearrange the seats for a reading plane after you have had a train for a month or two.

Rationale
1. Children who normally don't like to read may be motivated by this technique as you have turned reading into a fun game.
2. This is also an additional reward for completing assignments accurately.
3. Using key children as checkers can be of great help to the teacher, and helps to assure that only children who have completed their assignments ride the train.

READING TRAIN

Grades 1-3 / Improving Reading Skills

Reading Worm

Situation
You would like to encourage your class to read more books.

Strategy
1. Make the head of an attractive worm out of a paper plate and fasten it to a wall leaving room for the body of the worm.
2. Tell your children that it is a reading worm.
3. Indicate that each time a child reads a book the name of the book and the child's name will be recorded on a paper plate and the plate will serve as a segment of the worm's body.
4. Encourage the children to add many segments to the worm's body by reading many books.
5. Watch the worm grow around your room as the reading continues.
6. Take the paper plates down from the wall at the end of a few months. Give them to the children so they can take them home and show their parents the number of books they have read.
7. Serve each child a special treat on one of his or her paper plates.

Rationale
1. The segments give children a visual indication of the number of books they have read.
2. They are also encouraged to make the worm grow by reading.
3. They have an opportunity to show their success to their parents and to receive extra praise.

Grades 1-3 / Improving Reading Skills

The Read-O-Meter

Situation
Oksana is inattentive in reading classes and does not always complete her assignments. You want to motivate her to complete her assignments and to do them accurately.

Strategy
1. Draw a thermometer with twenty spaces. Call it a read-o-meter.
2. Tell Oksana that she may color in one space each day that her work is completed correctly and on time.
3. Encourage her to complete a space a day. Praise her daily.
4. When twenty spaces have been completed, let Oksana take the read-o-meter home. Praise her for completing twenty spaces. A treat might also be given to her at this time.

Rationale
1. The read-o-meter provides a student with a visual image of the progress made for twenty school days and tends to motivate the student to complete assignments correctly and on time.
2. Praise is often an effective positive reinforcer.
3. Additional praise that a student receives from parents acts as another reinforcer.

Grades 1-5 / Attention Seeking

The Return Of The Toys

Situation
Craig is a boy who brings toy cars to school and plays with them on his desk when he should be listening to class discussions and directions or completing his assigned work. You have taken many of his cars from him and have a drawer full of them, as well as some of his other toys. He also strives for attention.

Strategy
1. Make a contract with Craig. As part of the contract, he can get back his cars and toys provided he listens to directions and completes assignments instead of disturbing the class.
2. Have Craig earn points for completing work correctly during blocks of time throughout the school day.
3. Assign a point value to each toy. The higher points should be assigned to the toys he wants back the most, because he will work the hardest and for longer periods of time to obtain them.
4. Give him the car or toy that he has earned at the end of the day and let him take it home.
5. Give Craig an added bonus for earning points within a given time. A privilege that he really wants is a good bonus item.
6. When all of the cars or toys have been earned, switch to other privileges Craig can earn each day.

Rationale
1. This is an effective use of a point system.
2. It also uses toys that have value to the child and enables him to get them back and take them home. A child will usually modify his behavior to get back his toys.
3. A child feels good about getting his toys back and feels that the system and the teacher are fair.

4. As the child continues to improve his work, natural reinforcers may take over as his knowledge and skills increase; consequently, it may not be necessary to continue with extrinsic reinforcers.
5. Privileges can also be positive reinforcers.

Grades 2-5 / Inattentiveness

The Right Answer

Situation

You want to improve student attention and performance during classroom discussions.

Strategy
1. Plan to ask questions that reflect different aspects of difficulty so that all students will know the answers to at least some of the questions.
2. Have a child come up to you in front of the room for a handshake when a correct answer is given.

Rationale
1. A handshake will positively reinforce desirable behavior.
2. It will also be a positive reason for children to get out of their seats and move around the classroom.
3. Children usually develop better self-concepts when they give correct answers, and are proud of their correct responses.

Grades 2-4 / Improving Reading Skills

Rita's Toys

Situation
Rita is an intelligent girl. She does not read well. She dawdles and does not complete her assigned seatwork. All that she appears to want to do is to play with the toys that she has brought from home. You want her to read better, complete her assigned seatwork, and pay attention to directions.

Strategy
1. Make a contract with Rita stating that she may play with toys for ten minutes at the end of the morning if she has completed her seatwork accurately and has earned four points.
2. Divide the morning into four time blocks. Let her earn a point for work completed in each of the time blocks, marking each on the chalkboard.
3. When she has earned four points, let her play in back of the room with her toys for ten minutes. For an additional positive reinforcer let her choose a friend to play with in the back of the room. This will cause the children in the class to encourage Rita to complete her work throughout the morning so that one of them may play with her.

Rationale
1. Rita has a chance of being more productive if the time is broken into short periods rather than long ones.
2. Chalkboard marks provide a visual indication of earned points. Short time spans provide positive reinforcement throughout the morning.
3. The children put a premium on having Rita for a friend in the classroom, and cause Rita to develop socially as she increases the scope of her friendships.

Grades 4-6 / Inadequate Academic Performance

Rockets To The Moon

Situation
At the beginning of the school year your class is not performing academically in accordance with its potential. You would like to motivate each child to be more productive.

Strategy
1. Make a rocket for each child in your class.
2. Place the rockets in a row at the base of your bulletin board.
3. Place a moon for each rocket at the top of the bulletin board. Holes should be punched in the nose and tail of each of the rockets and another at the base of each moon.
4. Place vertical strings between each of the rockets and moons. Slip string through the holes in the rocket to enable the rocket to slide up the string on the way to the moon.
5. Cut some colored construction paper to make fifteen or twenty horizontal lines to serve as stages of progress.
6. Permit each child to move the rocket up one interval if all of the class assignments for a particular day have been completed satisfactorily.
7. As a bonus let a child move the rocket up two intervals for exceptional work on a given day.
8. Permit each child to have a prearranged positive reinforcer upon reaching the moon.
9. Give the class a bonus reinforcer when all children have reached their moons.

Rationale
1. This technique provides positive reinforcement on an individual basis.
2. Students can see their progress each day. This visualization will tend to reinforce students to work harder because their goals are always in sight.

3. This technique is also positive in nature because children can only move upward.
4. Giving a class a bonus will cause the children to encourage their peers to improve in performance.

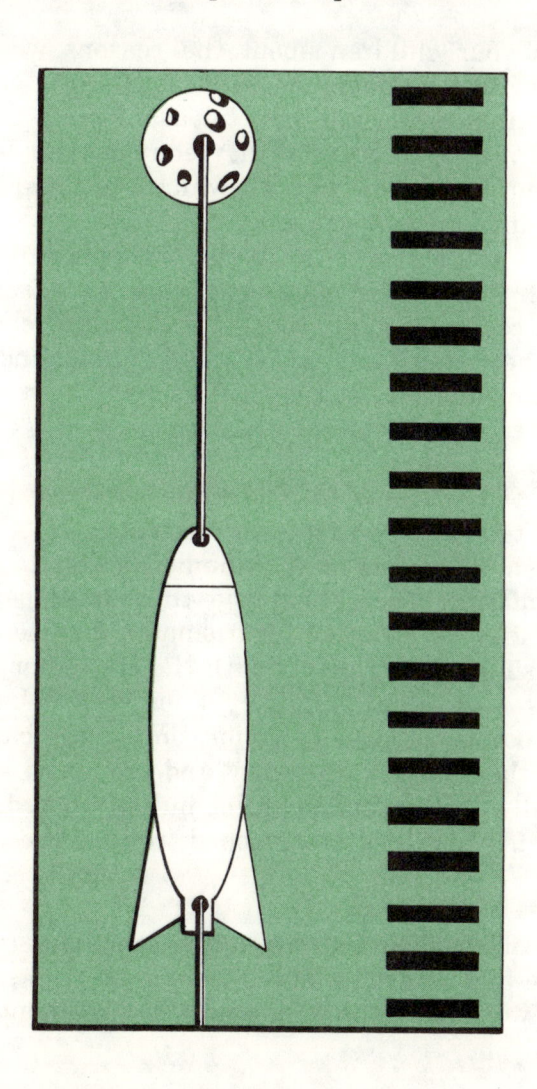

Grades 4-6 / Disruptive Behavior

School — A Pleasant Place To Work

Situation

Your class is acting out. They also have difficulty in following directions.

Strategy
1. Talk to your children about the reasons why they are acting in this manner.
2. Suggest that school can be a pleasant place to work and they may enjoy it more if they change their ways.
3. Ask them to list the ways in which the classroom can be restructured to make it more pleasant.
4. At times the children can be given opportunities to suggest items for their classroom, such as a sofa, rugs, a private corner, a game corner, and padded chairs or pillows. These items can be obtained secondhand.
5. Have the children list the positive reinforcers each would like to receive. Combine the lists into one class list in order of popular preference.
6. Permit the students to determine the way they should behave to merit positive reinforcement.
7. Establish 100 points as the number needed to receive the top reinforcer. The second and third most popular reinforcers may be awarded for a smaller number of points.
8. Establish a scale of points with the class. For example, 5 points for excellent behavior, 4 for good behavior, 3 for fair, 0 points for poor behavior, on a daily basis.
9. Award the points consistently and promptly; keep a running tally on the chalkboard or bulletin board. When the designated numbers are reached, reward the class.

Rationale
1. Each teacher should strive to make the classroom a comfortable and relaxed place.
2. Pupils work better in a pleasant environment.

Grades K-3 / Self-Image

School Phobia

Situation
Walter has "school phobia." He misses many days of school and is behind in his work. His entrance into the school is traumatic for both him and his mother. Once he gets into the classroom and settles down, he begins to work well. You want to reinforce his coming to school.

Strategy
1. Speak to the school nurse to suggest that the child's parents take him to their physician for an examination to determine whether or not his phobia has a physical basis.
2. If it is not physically based, have the parents take Walter to school and then leave him.
3. Let the parents know that they will be called if their presence is needed.
4. Get Walter involved in a school activity such as a game, reading a story, etc.
5. Praise Walter for coming to school and tell him how much you and your class have missed him.
6. Show Walter a calendar and tell him that he can mark an "X" on each date that he is in school. Encourage him to earn as many "Xs" as possible. Praise him every time he records an "X."
7. Encourage him to earn five "Xs" a week. You might also want to give him another positive reinforcer for such an accomplishment. An example might be to serve as the class messenger.
8. Let him take his calendar home each week for additional positive reinforcement from his parents. The parents could offer him an extra hour of television some night or any other kind of activity in which he might like to engage.

Rationale
1. Providing a visual chart will enable Walter to monitor his progress.
2. The "Xs" serve as daily and weekly positive reinforcers. As they start to accumulate, Walter tries to increase the number and comes to school.
3. Letting Walter know that he is missed by the other students will enhance his self-worth.

Grades 1-4 / Inadequate Academic Performance

Seat of Honor

Situation
You want to improve your children's work habits while they are being asked to work independently at their seats and while you are working with another group in front of the room.

Strategy
1. Make a "Seat of Honor" with a desk in a corner of your room.
2. Write the words "Seat of Honor" on the chalkboard as the children are working independently.
3. Write the name of a child on the chalkboard under the words "Seat of Honor" about every fifteen or thirty minutes. When you write a child's name at the chalkboard, it is a signal for a new child to work in the "Seat of Honor." Within a given day it may be possible for quite a few children to be given the privilege of working in the "Seat of Honor."
4. Give particular children a second chance from time to time for working in the "Seat of Honor." It will keep the ones with a tendency to misbehave working as well as others.

Rationale
1. Children need and enjoy recognition. In this technique they are being singled out for positive recognition.
2. A "Seat of Honor" can effectively motivate many children throughout the course of a school day.
3. Writing a child's name on the chalkboard for good behavior further tends to reinforce the desirable behavior.

Grades 1-2 / Disruptive Behavior

Seatwork

Situation
Don was observed to have a maximum attention span of ten minutes. He is an extremely anxious youngster who has little control over his own facilities. Usually his frustrations and his impulsive behavior are transferred into aggression. You are having a difficult time dealing with him.

Strategy
1. Have Don sit within your reach.
2. Give Don a red chip whenever he behaves satisfactorily for five minutes.
3. Isolate him for disruptive behavior.
4. Let Don take out his coloring book or programmed reading book when he has earned ten red chips.
5. Exchange each ten red chips for a blue chip. Ten blue chips should allow Don to visit the learning center to play a special game or use an audiovisual device, or have some unusual privilege within school boundaries.

Rationale
1. This system takes some effort on the teacher's part; however, it will require far more effort to cope with Don if nothing is done. Don could destroy the classroom dynamics. It would be wishful thinking to expect Don's behavior to improve if nothing is done.
2. Children who are like Don usually enjoy programmed reading because they may write in the book, and there are many picture clues. Pages can be finished quickly. There is also the immediate reinforcement that children receive when they mark their own work. They get the feel of reading many pages in a short amount of time. Moreover, much repetition is built into the system to insure success.
3. Don receives reinforcement from collecting chips.

Grades 1-3 / Improving Class Attitudes

Seatwork Ticket

Situation
Carmen dawdles and takes a while to start her reading seatwork. You want Carmen to develop a more positive attitude.

Strategy
1. Announce that the children may not return to their seats to work on a particularly "wonderful" paper without a ticket. Do this as a small reading group is finishing its oral work with the teacher.
2. Have each child answer a question correctly or perform a task that helps to review vocabulary or other parts of the lesson, before being issued a seatwork ticket.
3. Ask several of the children questions. As they give the correct responses let them return to their seats with their earned tickets.
4. Keep Carmen waiting until near the end, so that you are able to spend a bit more time with her.
5. Give Carmen a question that you know she can answer. Issue a ticket to her. Smile and say, "I know that you are going to have fun working at your seat today."

Rationale
1. This technique helps to effectively review the lesson.
2. It encourages a positive attitude toward schoolwork.

Grades K-3 / Incomplete Classwork

Shaping A Student

Situation

Instead of doing his seatwork Michael walks around the room for too long a period of time. You want Michael to sit down at his seat and complete his work.

Strategy
1. Realize that Michael's behavior needs to be shaped by being controlled.
2. Watch Michael's actions. When he comes near his seat say, "I like the way that Michael is standing near his seat."
3. This will usually stop Michael at his seat. Say next, "Michael looks good sitting at his seat."
4. Remark, "This is going to be a good day for Michael," when Michael sits down. "Look how well he holds his pencil. He is really going to work today."
5. Continue to positively reinforce Michael with praise throughout the morning or afternoon, or both, while he works at his seat.

Rationale
1. Shaping is an effective technique for changing the behavior of children who might otherwise not be changed.
2. Shaping utilizes praise for successive approximations until the actual goal is reached.
3. Shaping often helps students to get started in the right direction at the beginning of the school day and to keep them working.

Grades 5-6 / Social Skills

Showcase

Situation
Several students do not seem to be able to cooperate with each other. Their names are Tim, Sandy, Dan, Vince, and Connie.

Strategy
1. Explain that next week the class will be responsible for decorating the showcase for the school. This is an honor and a responsibility.
2. Select Tim, Sandy, Dan, Vince, and Connie for decorating the showcase.
3. Explain that they must prove to you that they can cooperate in the planning of the showcase before they will be permitted to execute the project.
4. Have the students show you the plan and the areas of responsibility of each member.
5. Permit them to complete the project if cooperation was shown in the planning.
6. Split them into small groups with other well-behaved youngsters if you think it is too risky to put all of these students together.

Rationale
1. Most buildings have a central showcase for the school or grade level. Students appreciate it and have their self-esteem enhanced when their own work is displayed before their peers or to the school.
2. The cooperation necessary to decorate the showcase necessitates good peer group relationships.
3. Peer group pressure will aid in the success of this project.
4. Children usually perform well when adults have confidence in them and offer them words of praise.

Grades 1-3 / Improving Class Attitudes

The Silver Carpet

Situation

You are going to show a motion picture to two or three classes in your room. You want to encourage good behavior during the showing of the films. You also have a limited number of seats in your room. You want some children to sit on the floor and feel good about it.

Strategy

1. Put some gray rag paper on the floor in your room where you need extra seating space.
2. Walk alongside the classes that are lining up outside your door to come inside.
3. Look at the children for a while and say nothing.
4. Say to the children, "I'm looking for the best-behaved children. I have a silver carpet in my room. The best-behaved children will be selected to sit on the silver carpet."
5. Select the students who exhibit the best behavior to sit upon the gray rag paper. Have all others sit in the seats.
6. State periodically, "I especially like the way the children are sitting on the silver carpet. There are also many children in the seats who are sitting quietly."

Rationale

1. This is a convenient technique for solving a seating problem. It places emphasis on proper behavior.
2. In the course of the year you should give many different children the opportunity to sit on the silver carpet. Praise also the children in the seats when they are behaving properly.

Grades K-3 / Maintaining Good Performance

Special Carrier For The Day

Situation
Wahkuna is an average girl doing average work. Because the size of the class is large and Wahkuna poses no particular problems she is being overlooked, seldom receiving any extra attention.

Strategy
1. Tell the class that Wahkuna is going to be your special carrier for a day because you like her behavior and the way she always completes her work.
2. This means that Wahkuna will be an errand runner, carrying your books, carrying the ball and other equipment out to recess, or carrying anything else that is lifted or moved throughout the day.
3. Choose another so-called average child the next day for the same kind of positive reinforcement.

Rationale
1. The average child is in the classroom approximately five to six hours a day. Often the teacher's time is devoted to those who deviate from the norm. Therefore, many teachers neglect the average or well-behaved student.
2. All children need attention and recognition. If they don't get it for desirable behavior then they will often seek it through undesirable behavior.
3. "Special Carrier for the Day" and other methods with the average child may be preventive in nature, as special recognition is given to the children who otherwise are unnoticed.

Grades 1-3 / Disruptive Behavior

Special Delivery

Situation

Johnnie gets restless after he has been in the classroom for two hours and has difficulty concentrating on his work assignments. He begins to engage in undesirable behavior.

Strategy
1. Watch Johnnie's behavior carefully for symptoms of inattentiveness to assigned tasks.
2. Put a book in a large envelope and send Johnnie to a prearranged room with the package before he starts to engage in undesirable behavior.
3. Have the teacher who receives the package thank and praise Johnnie.

Rationale
1. Leaving the room gives Johnnie a break from the demanding routine of the class in an acceptable manner.
2. Giving Johnnie something different to do while he is behaving satisfactorily minimizes the attention he gains for engaging in undesirable behavior, therefore desirable behavior should increase.

Grades 1-3 / Disruptive Behavior

The Squeeze

Situation
Consuelo is an angry, restless child who cannot work independently for long periods of time at her seat. She works for a while and then starts to eat candy, throw wads of paper at others, make noises, and take frequent trips to the pencil sharpener or the washroom. You want to keep her from disrupting your classroom. You want her to improve her academic performance.

Strategy
1. Have Consuelo read with her own group.
2. While she is reading with her own group, have her sit next to the teacher.
3. Reach over and squeeze her hand occasionally and smile at her so that she knows that you care about her and that she can get attention without being disruptive.
4. Put your hand on Consuelo's head or shoulder as a variation of the procedure.
5. Give her several chances for success with her own reading group so that she can start the morning enthusiastically.
6. Let her work on her seatwork. Tell her that she may work with another reading group if she completes her work on time.
7. Invite her to read with a slower group. Give her many opportunities for achieving status with the group, by reading correct answers or giving correct responses to questions dealing with comprehension.

Rationale
1. In this situation you are using a combination of positive reinforcers, touch, praise and proximity.
2. Consuelo is now able to gain attention without engaging in undesirable behavior.

Grades 1-3 / Tardiness And Absenteeism

Star On The Calendar

Situation
Brett is continually late for school. You want to reinforce his coming to school on time.

Strategy
1. Praise Brett when he comes to school on time.
2. Let him put a star on the calendar for each date that he is on time for school.
3. Provide an additional reinforcer for each time that he earns five stars.
4. Let him take the calendar home each week for additional reinforcement from home if the family is willing to cooperate.

Rationale
1. This technique gives Brett a positive reason for coming to school.
2. It gives the child a visual indication of his performance.
3. Keeping his own record helps Brett to develop responsibility for his actions and to feel good about his performance.

Grades 1-5 / Tardiness And Absenteeism

Surprise Bags

Situation

Your class has a 15% absentee rate. You have appealed to the parents to bring their children to school regularly, but too many people in this transient community have their personal problems and are uncooperative. There is little you can teach if the children don't come to school.

Strategy
1. Make weekly calendars for each child and post them either on their desks or in some other noticeable place.
2. Hand them a silver star to paste on their charts when they come to school in the morning. If a child gets five silver stars for perfect weekly attendance then the child may choose from your Silver Star Surprise Bag that contains small items, such as trinkets, etc. If more than half of the students in your class have perfect attendance for the week, give your class an extra privilege.
3. Send the students with perfect weekly attendance to the principal, counselor, nurse, or another teacher with their charts. Have that person shake their hands.
4. Give a big gold star and choice of items from the Gold Star Bag to anyone with perfect attendance for the month. This bag has even more interesting reinforcers than the Silver Star Surprise Bag. Try to obtain money from your local school organization or get contributions to fill your surprise bags.

Rationale
1. The element of surprise as in "Surprise Bag" is often effective with children.
2. Poor students have as good a chance of being successful as good students.
3. Children work hard to obtain real rewards.

Grades 5-6 / Self-Image

Tall Alex

Situation

Alex is a tall, lanky boy. The students make fun of his size and awkwardness. He stoops over because he feels self conscious about his height. You want to improve his posture and his feelings about himself.

Strategy

1. Say to Alex in front of the class, "My, you are so tall. Isn't that wonderful? Aren't you lucky? I'll bet that you're going to be a tall basketball player who will make a lot of points for the junior high and senior high school teams. Our team can always use tall players."
2. Say also, "Tall players walk tall, run tall, jump high."
3. Note every time Alex walks tall and say, "Alex looks like a basketball player. See how tall he walks."
4. On one of your walls, make a vertical line that is 8 feet high. Divide it into 6-inch segments.
5. Have Alex and the other students practice jumping to ascertain how high they can reach. Praise the students who jump the highest.
6. Mark each student's record on the wall by writing each name at the spot touched.
7. If during observation of jumping practice it appears that Alex will be a loser because of his awkwardness, then you may want to add a stretch contest to see which students reach the highest. Thus Alex is sure to win.

Rationale

1. Alex is a winner for a change. Winning in competition can be highly reinforcing, especially to a child who is often a loser.
2. Praise and the attention Alex will receive from his classmates serve as a positive reinforcer and may enhance his social interaction with them.

113

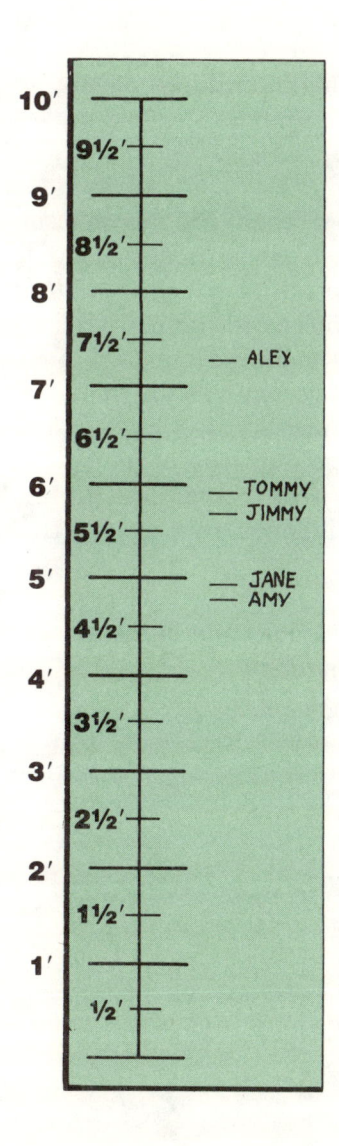

10'
9½'
9'
8½'
8'
7½' — ALEX
7'
6½'
6' — TOMMY
— JIMMY
5½'
5' — JANE
— AMY
4½'
4'
3½'
3'
2½'
2'
1½'
1'
½'

Grades K-1 / Inadequate Academic Performance

Telephone Poles, Trees, And Houses

Situation
Many of your kindergarten children do not know their names, addresses, and phone numbers.

Strategy
1. Tell your children that you are going to start a new bulletin board with trees, houses, and telephone poles.
2. Put a tree on the bulletin board with each child's name as he or she learns to recognize it.
3. Put a house on the bulletin board near the appropriate tree as each child recognizes his or her address. Mark the address on the house.
4. Put a telephone pole on the other side of the house from the tree as each child recognizes his or her phone number. Mark the telephone number on the pole.

Rationale
1. This technique provides the children with a visual image of their accomplishments.
2. It permits them to be reinforced for learning three different concepts.
3. It provides you with an interesting bulletin board.

JACK

ANDY

16 Nelson Avenue

JOE

2501 Maryland Avenue

RANDY

BOB

209 Orange Road

657-8800

115

Grades 5-6 / Attention Seeking

Thelma's Call

Situation
Thelma is a new student, recently transferred from another school in your district. She is misbehaving in many ways: showing off, fighting, yelling out in class, etc. You have tried various strategies with her: praise, kindness, and strict discipline, but nothing seems to work. You want to change her general behavior.

Strategy
1. Structure Thelma on a system that will give her a ticket at set intervals for good behavior. Attempt to change only the behavior that annoys you the most.
2. Encourage Thelma to go to the office and call whomever she chooses from her previous school: a teacher, counselor, principal, cafeteria worker, etc. This should be done when she receives a designated number of tickets. Thelma should be instructed in how to tell the person she won a certain number of tickets for doing well in school.
3. Continue the system, but have the phone calls reversed: notify the involved person at the other school when Thelma has ten points and have that person call Thelma and congratulate her.
4. Call Thelma's parents when she has reached the goal you set up for her.

Rationale
1. A telephone call to her former school can have great reinforcement value for a girl like Thelma, particularly when it is for the purpose of reporting good behavior.
2. The telephone call also suggests Thelma now needs to live up to the new image she is creating.
3. It helps to program Thelma into the direction of good behavior.

Grades 2-4 / Incomplete Classwork

Time For Yourself

Situation
You are working with a reading group. Shawn has seatwork assigned to him. He does not complete his seatwork. He stares into space, makes noises, and throws erasers, paper wads, pencils, and crayons at others.

Strategy
1. Find out the things that Shawn likes to do. This can be done through observation or merely by asking him. Have Shawn rank them according to importance. Put a point value on each. The highest points should be set for the tasks he enjoys the most, because those are the ones for which he will work the hardest to attain.
2. Suggest to Shawn that he might have time to do some of the things he likes if he completes his assigned tasks.
3. Make a contract with Shawn, giving him the right to engage in activities that he likes, contingent upon the performance of assigned tasks.
4. Set up blocks of time as part of the contract. Give Shawn a point if assigned tasks are performed during given time parameters, such as 9:00 - 9:30 A.M.
5. Have Shawn count up the number of points he has earned at the end of the morning and permit him to engage in activities that are in line with the points he has earned.
6. Do the same for the afternoon. Bonus activities might be permitted if Shawn earns a given number of points within a given week.

Rationale
1. Giving a child the privilege of doing what he or she likes can cause the child to perform less enjoyable tasks.
2. By having a child work on eliminating one form of undesirable behavior others may disappear in the process.

Grades 1-3 / Improving Mathematics Skills

Token In The Can

Situation
You want to improve your children's attention span and performance in mathematics while working with number facts.

Strategy
1. Put a small decorated frozen juice can on the upper right-hand corner of each pupil's desk.
2. Put a token (like a poker chip) into the can when a child makes a correct response.
3. Have the children count their tokens at the end of the morning, and cash them in for privileges or items from a table of reinforcers.
4. Have the children use the items during recess.
5. Have them use the privileges at specified times during the day.

Rationale
1. Tokens can have positive reinforcement value, particularly if items and privileges can be purchased with the tokens.
2. Each time a child gets a token, it suggests that something positive or worthwhile has been accomplished.
3. Children often cannot wait for long range rewards. The immediate reinforcement used in this technique is usually effective and will move the child in the direction of earning the greater reinforcer.

Grades 1-3 / Inattentiveness

The Touch

Situation
Leilani is a girl who is lazy and inattentive. You want to improve her classroom performance.

Strategy
1. Observe Leilani's oral and written work.
2. Praise her when her performance is better than usual.
3. Put the palm of your hand on the top of her head firmly and say, "I am really pleased with you."
4. If her performance has not been good, give Leilani an assignment in which she can succeed. It will also give you reasons to praise her.

Rationale
1. The praise that you give Leilani may make a difference in her performance.
2. The "Touch" is the dual reinforcer which makes this technique even more effective.
3. You are conveying to Leilani the idea that you appreciate her positive behavior, and you like her as an individual.

Grades 3-5 / Disruptive Behavior

Two Drinks

Situation

The water fountain is in the hallway and the children are constantly asking the teacher if they may get a drink. Some children are taking advantage of the situation. You would like better control over this problem.

Strategy
1. Place two math problems on the chalkboard, preferably after you have introduced a new concept.
2. Place a student's name, as well as two circles, beside the math problems you are presenting. Do this in the morning.

   NED   527   625
   ◯ ◯ × 48 × 24

3. For example, tell Ned that when he finishes a problem correctly he should put an "X" inside a circle, and then he may get a drink.
4. Follow the same procedure in the afternoon, presenting another problem and having each child put an "X" inside a circle after successfully completing a problem. The "Xs" help to keep track of students who have been to the fountain.

Rationale
1. Children feel proud and worthy when they earn a reward. Most children would rather earn a reward than be given one.
2. Children tend to be motivated by short term rewards, in this case, the drink.
3. It is likely they will be more accurate on their math problems if getting the problem correct is the key to getting a drink.

Grades K-2 / Attention Seeking

Visit The Nurse

Situation
Dernon is a child who defecates in his underwear each day. His father recently passed away and his mother is forced to work in order to support the family. Dernon does not get the attention he once received. He is a most anxious boy. You send Dernon to the nurse to be changed each time he defecates in his underwear. You find that his condition is not improving because he is enjoying the added attention and physical contact from the nurse.

Strategy
1. Insist that Dernon be given a complete physical examination to rule out natural causes for his condition. If there does not appear to be a natural cause for his condition, try a program of behavior modification.
2. Have Dernon's mother send you several changes of underwear.
3. Send Dernon to the lavatory to change himself after each accident.
4. Tell Dernon that he may visit the nurse for ten minutes at the end of the day if he has not soiled himself.
5. Have the nurse praise Dernon and give him special attention for maintaining clean underwear.

Rationale
1. Children will perform many acts to gain attention and recognition.
2. Dernon was undoubtedly using an inappropriate form of behavior to get attention.
3. The nurse was the agent who first reinforced Dernon's undesirable responses, but was later used to help him learn more accepted forms of behavior.

BONUS APPLICATIONS

The authors are firm believers in behavior modification that utilizes positive reinforcers to increase the frequency of desirable behaviors. Consequently, to reinforce the readers who have completed the first one hundred applications, five additional applications have been included. It is hoped that the bonus applications will be of further value to teachers in their daily contact with children.

Grades 1-3 / Incomplete Classwork

Walking With The Principal

Situation
Marilyn does not get her work done. She annoys other children. She steals from them. She talks out of turn and tries to get your attention in undesirable ways. You want her to complete her work. You hope that while she gets her work done, she will not disturb others.

Strategy
1. Make a contract with Marilyn which states that she may walk around the building with the principal at 10:30 A.M. and 2:30 P.M. when he or she is making a daily inspection of the building.
2. Make the contract contingent upon the completion of all work that has been assigned to her. Have her bring her completed work to the school secretary at 10:30 A.M., at noon, at 2:30 P.M., and after school. Have the secretary praise her for the completed work.
3. Have the principal also praise her for her completed assignments and take her on a tour of the building twice a day.

Rationale
1. Walking with the principal can be a positive reinforcer as it is a status symbol and a pleasant experience.
2. Marilyn may find the total school atmosphere more reinforcing than the activities of her classroom.
3. Marilyn now has a purpose for finishing her work.
4. Marilyn should now succeed as she has several people supporting her.

Grades 2-4 / Incomplete Classwork

Win Your Name

Situation
Todd is not completing his work. His attention span is very brief. You would like Todd to be more productive.

Strategy
1. Plan to give Todd a ticket or chip for each time he finishes a task.
2. Make a contract with Todd. When Todd receives two tickets or chips he turns them in to the teacher for the first letter of his name. The letter is large and in color.
3. Hang the letter in a noticeable place in the classroom.
4. Continue the process until Todd completes his full name.
5. Reward the class or Todd, depending on what is stipulated in the contract, when Todd wins his full name.
6. Praise Todd and tell him how nice his name looks in front of the class and how proud you are that he was able to win his own name.
7. Continue this practice until Todd is able to do his work independently without the positive reinforcer.
8. A variation of this technique is to cut out two letters and send the duplicate home when Todd finishes a task. Be sure to orient Todd's parents concerning your plan so they can also display his name as well as reinforce him when his name is completed.

Rationale
1. You are giving Todd the recognition he needs for desirable behavior so he won't attempt to get recognition for undesirable behavior.
2. Making Todd feel good about his name should help him to feel proud of himself. A good self-concept usually has a carry-over into all areas of learning and behavior.
3. Changing only one behavior at a time gives Todd a good chance to succeed in this technique.

Grades 2-4 / Improving Class Attitudes

Work At The Teacher's Desk

Situation
Poor general discipline in your class prevents optimum learning. You would like to improve your classroom climate.

Strategy
1. Tell the class that you will be selecting a "Student of the Hour" based on hard work and good behavior.
2. Each hour, pick your "Student of the Hour."
3. Issue that student a pass that reads, "Good for fifteen minutes at the teacher's desk." This can be turned in at any time the student selects. If the teacher's desk has two writing leaves, then two students can work there at the same time.

Rationale
1. Children like recognition. Sitting at the teacher's desk singles them out and gives them positive recognition.
2. The teacher is an adult and a leader. Therefore, most children feel grown-up and important sitting at the teacher's desk.
3. Desirable behavior can be positively reinforced with this approach.

Grades 2-5 / Disruptive Behavior

"X" On The Calendar

Situation
Anaba engages in undesirable behavior that is disruptive to the class.

Strategy
1. Make a contract with Anaba permitting her to mark her good behavior on a calendar.
2. Indicate to Anaba that if she engages in proper behavior for the morning she may mark a diagonal line on the calendar for that date. If she engages in proper behavior for the afternoon she may make a second diagonal on the date, forming the letter "X." If she earns "Xs" for an entire week, she may take the calendar to the principal.
3. Give her verbal praise when she marks a diagonal.
4. The principal should praise Anaba when she comes to the office.
5. Give Anaba an opportunity to take the calendar home each week, or if necessary, each night, so that the parents can have a current record of her behavior and provide additional reinforcement.

Rationale
1. Multiple reinforcement is used in this strategy: the first diagonal, the second diagonal, the "X" on the calendar, and praise from the teacher, principal, and parents.
2. This procedure programs a child toward success. It is accomplished through a series of steps.

Grades 5-6 / Disruptive Behavior

Yea Martin!

Situation
Martin uses many undesirable behaviors that are destroying the class dynamics. Examples are calling out, hitting others, tipping over school furniture, and using profanity.

Strategy
1. Talk to the class about Martin's behavior in his presence. Say to the class, "I think that Martin has the *guts* to behave like a high school boy."
2. Ask the class to support Martin in his effort to change his behavior.
3. Put a letter on the board for every fifteen minutes of Martin's appropriate behavior. After Martin behaves appropriately for nine periods, the chalkboard should appear as follows:

YEA MARTIN!

4. Have the children say, "Yea Martin!" three times when Martin's name has been spelled out. Then have Martin choose a reinforcer that can be shared by all members of the class. Examples: extra recess, games, dramatic play.
5. Lengthen the required period of time for a letter for the board to twenty minutes, and then to thirty minutes as Martin succeeds in accomplishing his goal.

Rationale
1. It is apparent that Martin needs attention. Give it to him for desirable rather than undesirable behavior.
2. This procedure rallies the peer group in support of Martin and heightens his self-esteem, particularly when the group shouts, "Yea Martin!"
3. Short intervals of time give Martin an excellent chance for success in quickly accumulating enough letters to earn a reinforcement to share with others.

SUGGESTED READINGS

Some readers of this book may become interested in the theory behind the concept of behavior modification; others may become interested in extending and expanding the practical applications of the concept. In either case, the titles listed on the next two pages should prove useful for those who want to know more about behavior modification.

Suggested Readings

The following books and articles are suggested for those who are interested in reading more about behavior modification.

Allport, F.H., *Social Psychology*. Cambridge, MA: Riverside Press, 1924.

Ayllon, T., & Azrin, N.H. *Token Economy: A Motivational System For Therapy And Rehabilitation*. New York: Appleton-Century-Crofts, 1968.

Bandura, A. *Principles Of Behavior Modification*. New York: Holt, Rinehart and Winston, 1969.

Bandura, A. & Walters, R.H. *Adolescent Aggression*. New York: Ronald Press, 1959.

Bandura, A., & Walters, R.H. *Social Learning And Personality Development*. New York: Holt, Rinehart and Winston, 1963.

Braun, Bertram. *Behavior Modification*. Rockville, MD: U.S. Department of Health, Education and Welfare, National Institute of Mental Health, 1975.

Eysenck, H.J. *Experiments In Behavior Therapy*. New York: Pergamon, 1964.

Fischer, Joel. *Planned Behavior Change*. New York: Free Press, 1975.

Kazdin, Arthur W. *Behavior Modification In Applied Settings*. Homewood, IL: Dorsey Press, 1975.

Lawrence, D.H., & Festinger, L. *Deterrents And Reinforcement: The Psychology Of Insufficient Reward*. Palo Alto, CA: Stanford University Press, 1962.

Macmillan, Donald. *Behavior Modification In Education*. New York: Macmillan, 1973.

Madsen, Clifford and Charles Madsen. *Parents & Children, Love & Discipline: A Positive Approach*. Boston, MA: A.H.M., 1972.

Pavlov, I.P. *Conditioned Reflexes*. London: Oxford University Press, 1927.

Pizzat, Frank. *Behavior Modification In Residential Treatment For Children*. New York: Human Science Press, 1973.

Skinner, B.F. *Beyond Freedom And Dignity*. New York: Alfred A. Knopf, 1971.

Skinner, B.F. *Science And Human Behavior*. New York: The Macmillan Company, 1953.

Skinner, B.F. *The Technology Of Teaching*. Englewood Cliffs, NJ: Prentice-Hall, Inc., 1968.

Skinner, B.F. *Verbal Behavior. "Personality Theories."* New York: Appleton-Century-Crofts, 1957.

Strain, Phillip S., *Teaching Exceptional Children*. New York: Academic Press, 1976.

Ullman, L.P. and Krasner, L., Eds. *Research In Behavior Modification*. New York: Holt, Rinehart and Winston, 1965.

Ulrich, R., T. Stachnik, and J. Mabry. *Control Of Human Behavior*. Glenview, IL: Scott, Foresman, Volume I, 1966; Volume II, 1970.

Welch, Michael. *The Open Token Economy System*. Springfield, IL: Thomas, 1974.

1 2 3 4 5 6 7 8 9 – PP – 82 81 80 79 78